HONDA

XR75 SINGLES • 1975-1978

SERVICE • REPAIR • PERFORMANCE

By
ED SCOTT

ERIC JORGENSEN
Editor

JEFF ROBINSON
Publisher

CLYMER PUBLICATIONS

World's largest publisher of books devoted exclusively to automobiles and motorcycles.

12860 MUSCATINE STREET • P.O. BOX 20 • ARLETA, CALIFORNIA 91331

FIRST EDITION
First Printing July, 1978
Second Printing October, 1978

Printed in U.S.A.

ISBN: 0-89287-215-1

MOTORCYCLE INDUSTRY COUNCIL

Performance Improvement chapter by Chris Bunch

•

Cover photo by Mike Brown, Visual Imagery, Los Angeles, California

Chapter One
General Information

1

Chapter Two
Troubleshooting

2

Chapter Three
Basic Hand Tools

3

Chapter Four
Tune-up, Lubrication, and Maintenance

4

Chapter Five
Engine, Clutch, and Transmission

5

Chapter Six
Fuel, Ignition, and Exhaust Systems

6

Chapter Seven
Wheels and Brakes

7

Chapter Eight
Steering, Suspension, and Frame

8

Chapter Nine
Performance Improvement

9

Index

10

CONTENTS

QUICK REFERENCE DATA VII

CHAPTER ONE

GENERAL INFORMATION 1

Manual organization   Parts replacement
Service hints   Expendable supplies
Safety first   Serial numbers

CHAPTER TWO

TROUBLESHOOTING 6

Operating requirements   Clutch
Emergency troubleshooting   Brakes
Engine starting problems   Transmission
Operating problems   Suspension

CHAPTER THREE

BASIC HAND TOOLS 11

Fasteners   Torque wrench
Screwdrivers   Impact driver
Pliers   Ignition gauge
Box and open-end wrenches   Tire lever
Adjustable (crescent) wrenches   Spoke wrench
Socket wrenches   Tune-up and troubleshooting tools
Strap wrench   Mechanic's tips

CHAPTER FOUR

TUNE-UP, LUBRICATION, AND MAINTENANCE 20

Engine tune-up   Periodic lubrication
Lubricants   Periodic maintenance
Routine checks   Storage
Cleaning solvents

CHAPTER FIVE

ENGINE, CLUTCH, AND TRANSMISSION 38

Engine principles
Engine cooling
Servicing engine in frame
Engine
Cylinder head
Valves and valve seats
Camshaft and rocker assemblies
Cylinder
Piston and connecting rod
Piston rings

Primary drive
Clutch
Oil pump
Shifter mechanism
Magneto
Crankcase
Transmission
Gearshift drum and forks
Break-in
Specifications

CHAPTER SIX

FUEL, IGNITION, AND EXHAUST SYSTEMS 88

Carburetor
Fuel shutoff valve

Ignition system
Exhaust system

CHAPTER SEVEN

WHEELS AND BRAKES 96

Front wheel
Rear wheel
Brake cable
Brake lining

Brake drum
Drive chain
Tires and tubes
Tire repairs

CHAPTER EIGHT

STEERING, SUSPENSION, AND FRAME 108

Handlebars
Steering head
Front forks
Rear shocks
Swing arm

Kickstand (side stand)
Footpegs
Frame
Specifications

CHAPTER NINE

PERFORMANCE IMPROVEMENT 122

The most from stock
Planning performance
Suspension

Engine
Overall
Sources

INDEX 145

QUICK REFERENCE DATA

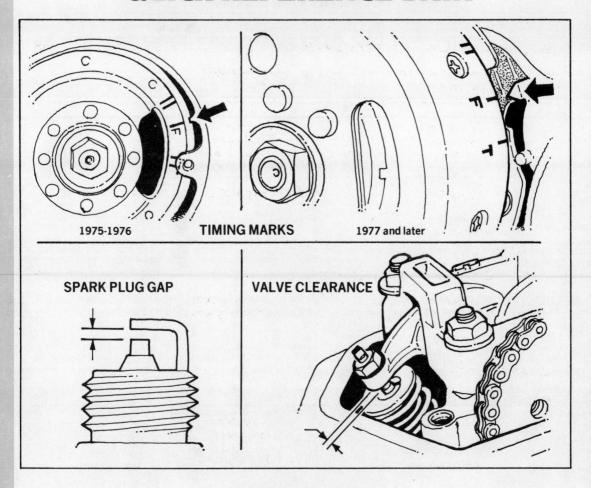

1975-1976 **TIMING MARKS** **1977 and later**

SPARK PLUG GAP **VALVE CLEARANCE**

TUNE-UP SPECIFICATIONS

Camshaft holder nuts	6-9 ft.-lb. (7-12 N•m)
Valve clearance (cold)	
Intake	0.002 in. (0.05mm)
Exhaust	0.002 in. (0.05mm)
Spark plug	
Type	NGK C7HS, ND U22FS
Gap	0.024-0.028 in. (0.6-0.7mm)
Contact point gap	0.012-0.016 in. (0.3-0.4mm)
Idle speed	1,400 ± 100 rpm

FLUIDS

Item	Type	Quantity
Engine oil		
All temperature	SAE 10W-40	0.9 U.S. qt. (0.9 liter)
Above 60°F (15°C)	SAE 20W-50	0.9 U.S. qt. (0.9 liter)
Fork oil	Automatic transmission fluid (ATF)	3.7 oz. (110cc)
Drive chain	SAE 30 engine oil or special chain lube	As needed
Fuel		
1975	Premium	1.2 U.S. gal. (4.5 liter)
1976-1978	Premium	0.8 U.S. gal. (3.0 liter)

CARBURETOR SPECIFICATIONS

Item	1975	1976-1978
Main jet	100	100
Air jet	150	150
Needle jet	0.1024 in. (2.6mm)	0.1024 in. (2.6mm)
Slow jet	38	35
Float level	0.827 in. (21mm)	0.7874 in. (20mm)

FRAME TORQUE SPECIFICATIONS

Item	Foot pounds (ft.-lb.)	Newton meters (N•m)
Steering stem nut	43-65	58-88
Handlebar holder	6-9	8-12
Front fork lower bridge bolts	14-22	19-30
Front axle nut	29-40	39-54
Rear axle nut	29-40	39-54
Rear brake torque arm	7-14	9-19
Rear fork pivot bolt	22-29	30-39
Rear shock absorber nuts	22-29	30-39
Rear brake arm	6-9	8-12
Foot peg assembly	14-22	19-30
Engine mounting bolts	14-22	19-30
Engine mounting plate bolts	11-18	15-24
Shift and kickstarter levers	6-9	8-12
Spokes	1-1.5	1.5-2.0

ENGINE TORQUE SPECIFICATIONS

Item	Foot pounds (ft.-lb.)	Newton meters (N•m)
Crankcase and engine side covers	5-9	7-12
Cam cover	6-9	8-12
Camshaft holder	6-9	8-12
Intake manifold	6-9	8-12
Magneto rotor	22-28	30-38
Oil filter rotor	25-33	34-45
Valve clearance adjuster nut	5-8	7-11
Cam sprocket bolts	7-12	9-16
Engine oil drain plug	15-22	20-30

TIRES

Front pressure	17 psi (1.2 kg/sq.cm)
Rear pressure	20 psi (1.4 kg/sq.cm)
Size	
Front	2.50-16 (4PR)
Rear	3.00-14 (4PR)

HONDA

XR75 SINGLES • 1975-1978

SERVICE • REPAIR • PERFORMANCE

CHAPTER ONE

GENERAL INFORMATION

This book provides maintenance and repair information for the Honda XR75 motorcycle. **Tables 1 and 2** provide general specifications and dimensions.

Maintenance and repair is not difficult if you know what tools to use and what to do. Anyone not afraid to get his or her hands dirty, of average intelligence, and with enough mechanical ability to change a light bulb can perform most of the procedures in this book.

In some cases, a repair job may require tools or skills not reasonably expected of the home mechanic. These instances are noted in each chapter and it is recommended that you take the job to your dealer, competent mechanic, or machine shop.

MANUAL ORGANIZATION

This manual provides service information and instructions for your Honda. All dimensions and capacities are expressed in English units familiar to U.S. mechanics as well as in metric units.

This chapter provides general information and specifications.

Chapter Two provides methods and suggestions for quick and accurate diagnosis and repair of problems. Troubleshooting procedures discuss typical and logical methods to pinpoint the trouble.

Chapter Three explains selection and use of tools you will need to work on the motorcycle.

Chapter Four explains tune-up procedures, periodic lubrication, and routine maintenance necessary to keep your bike running in top condition.

Subsequent chapters describe specific systems such as the engine, clutch, transmission, wheels, brakes and suspension. Each provides disassembly, repair, and assembly procedures in simple step-by-step form. If repair is impractical for a home mechanic, it is so indicated. It is usually faster and less expensive to take such repairs to a dealer or competent repair shop.

Some of the procedures in this manual specify special tools. In all cases, the tool is illustrated either in actual use or alone. A well-equipped mechanic may find that he can substitute similar tools already on hand or that he can fabricate his own.

The terms NOTE, CAUTION, and WARNING have specific meanings in this manual. A NOTE provides additional information to make a step or procedure easier or clearer. Disregarding a NOTE could cause inconvenience, but would not cause damage or personal injury.

A CAUTION emphasizes areas where equipment damage could result. Disregarding a CAUTION could cause permanent equipment damage; however, personal injury is unlikely.

Table 1   GENERAL SPECIFICATIONS

Engine type	Air-cooled, 4-stroke, OHC, single cylinder	
Bore and stroke		
1975-1976	1.850 x 1.630 in. (47.0 x 41.4mm)	
1977 and later	1.889 x 1.629 in. (48.0 x 41.4mm)	
Displacement		
1975-1976	4.4 cu. in. (72cc)	
1977 and later	4.57 cu. in. (74.9cc)	
Compression ratio		
1975-1976	8.8:1	
1977 and later	9.5:1	
Ignition	Flywheel magneto	
Lubrication	Wet sump, filter, oil pump	
Clutch	Wet, multi-plate (3)	
Transmission		
1975-1976	4-speed, constant mesh	
1977 and later	5-speed, constant mesh	
Transmission ratios	**1975-1976:**	**1977 and later:**
1st	2.500	2.690
2nd	1.722	1.820
3rd	1.333	1.400
4th	1.041	1.130
5th	—	0.960
Final reduction	3.142	3.285
Starting system	Kick-start	
Oil capacity	0.9 quart (0.9 liter)	
Fuel capacity		
1975	1.2 gallon (4.5 liter)/reserve: 0.3 gal. (1.0 liter)	
1976	0.8 gallon (3.0 liter)/reserve: 0.3 gal. (1.0 liter)	
1977 and later	0.8 gallon (3.0 liter)/reserve: 0.2 gal. (0.8 liter)	
Steering head angle	62° 50'	
Trail		
1975-1976	3.2 in. (82mm)	
1977 and later	3.07 in. (78mm)	
Front suspension	Telescopic fork	
1975-1976	4.1 in. (104mm)	
1977 and later	4.96 in. (126mm)	
Rear suspension	Swing arm, adjustable shock absorber	
1975-1976	2.4 in. (62mm)	
1977 and later	3.33 in. (84.6mm)	
Front tire	2.50-16 (4PR)	
Rear tire	3.00-14 (4PR)	

A WARNING emphasizes areas where personal injury or even death could result from negligence. Mechanical damage may also occur. WARNINGS are to be taken seriously. In some cases, serious injury or death has resulted from disregarding similar warnings.

Throughout this manual, keep in mind two conventions. "Front" refers to the front of the bike. The front of any component, such as the engine, is the end which faces toward the front of the bike. The left and right side refer to a person sitting on the seat facing forward. For example, the clutch/transmission is on the right side. These rules are simple, but even experienced mechanics occasionally become disoriented.

SERVICE HINTS

Most of the service procedures covered are straightforward and can be performed by

Table 2 GENERAL DIMENSIONS

	1975-1976	1977 and later
Overall length	65.7 in. (1670mm)	67 in. (1700mm)
Overall width	29 in. (740mm)	29.5 in. (750mm)
Overall height	37.4 in. (950mm)	39.7 in. (1010mm)
Wheelbase	44.9 in. (1140mm)	45 in. (1143mm)
Seat height	26.6 in. (675mm)	28.5 in. (725mm)
Footrest height	9.4 in. (240mm)	10.6 in. (270mm)
Ground clearance	6.7 in. (170mm)	7.4 in. (188mm)
Dry weight	141 lb. (64kg)	147.6 lb. (67kg)

anyone reasonably handy with tools. it is suggested, however, that you consider your own capabilities carefully before attempting any operation involving major disassembly of the engine.

Some operations, for example, require the use of a hydraulic press. It would be wiser to have these performed by a shop equipped for such work, rather than try to do the job yourself with makeshift equipment.

There are many items available that can be used on your hands before and after working on your bike. A little preparation prior to getting "all greased up" will help cleaning up later.

Before starting on your task, work Vaseline, soap, or a commercially available product, like ProTek, into your hands and under your fingernails and cuticles. This will make cleanup a lot easier.

For cleanup, use a waterless hand soap, like Sta-Lube, and then finish up with powdered Boraxo and a fingernail brush.

Repairs go much easier and faster if your bike is clean before you begin work. There are special cleaners, like Gunk Cycle Degreaser, for washing the engine and related parts. Follow the manufacturer's instructions. Clean all oily or greasy parts with cleaning solvent as you remove them.

WARNING
Never use gasoline as a cleaning solvent. It presents an extreme fire hazard. Be sure to work in a well-ventilated area when using cleaning solvent. Keep a fire extinguisher, rated for gasoline fires, handy in any case.

Special tools are required for some repairs. These may be purchased from a dealer, rented from a tool rental dealer, or fabricated by a mechanic or machinist, often at a considerable savings.

Much of the labor charge for repairs made by dealers is for the removal and disassembly of other parts to reach the defective unit. It is frequently possible to perform the preliminary operations yourself and then take the defective unit to the dealer for repair at considerable savings.

Once you have decided to tackle the job yourself, read the entire section in this manual which pertains to it. Study the illustrations, photos, and text until you have a good idea of what is involved in completing the job satisfactorily. If special tools are required, make arrangements to get them before you start. It is frustrating and time consuming to get partly into a job and then be unable to complete it.

During disassembly of parts, keep a few general cautions in mind. Force is rarely needed to get things apart. If parts have a tight fit, like a bearing in a case, there is usually a tool designed to separate them Never use a screwdriver to pry apart parts with machined surfaces such as crankcase halves. You will mar the surfaces and end up with leaks.

Make drawings and diagrams whenever similar-appearing parts are found. For instance, the engine crankcase bolts are of different lengths. You may think you can remember where everything came from — but mistakes could be costly. There is also the possibility that you may be side-tracked and not return to work for days or even weeks — in which interval, carefully laid out parts may have become disturbed.

Tag all similar internal parts for location and mark all mating parts for position. Record numbers and thickness of any shims as they are removed. Small parts, such as bolts, can be identified by placing them in plastic sandwich bags. Seal and label with masking tape.

Wiring should be tagged with masking tape and marked as each wire is removed. Again, do not rely on memory alone. Protect finished surfaces from physical damage or corrosion. Keep gasoline off painted surfaces.

Frozen or very tight bolts and screws can often be loosened by soaking them with penetrating oil, like Liquid Wrench or WD-40, then sharply striking the bolt head a few times with a hammer and punch (or screwdriver for screws). Avoid heat unless absolutely necessary since it may melt, warp, or remove the temper from many parts.

Avoid flames or sparks when working near flammable liquids such as gasoline.

No parts, except those assembled with a press fit, require force during assembly. If a part is hard to remove or install, find out why before proceeding.

Cover all openings after removing parts to keep dirt, small tools, etc., from falling in.

When assembling two parts, start all fasteners, then tighten evenly. Use tightening sequence as indicated in some of the procedures.

Wiring connections and brake shoes should be kept clean and free of grease and oil.

When assembling parts, be sure all shims and washers are replaced exactly as they came out.

Whenever a rotating part butts against a stationary part, look for a shim or washer. Use new gaskets if there is any doubt about the condition of the old ones. Generally you should apply gasket cement to one mating surface only so the parts may be disassembled in the future. A thin coat of oil on the gaskets helps them seal effectively.

Heavy grease can be used to hold small parts in place if they tend to fall out during assembly. However, keep grease and oil away from electrical components and brake parts.

Carburetors are best cleaned by disassembling them and soaking the parts in a commercial carburetor cleaner. Never soak gaskets or plastic or rubber parts in these cleaners. Never use wire to clean out the jet and air passages; they are easily damaged. Use compressed air to blow out the carburetor only if the float has been removed first.

Take your time and do the job right; do not forget that a newly rebuilt engine must be broken in the same as a new one.

SAFETY FIRST

Professional mechanics can work for years and never sustain a serious injury. If you observe a few rules of common sense and safety, you can enjoy many safe hours servicing your own motorcycle. You could hurt yourself or damage the bike if you ignore these rules.

1. Never use gasoline as a cleaning solvent.

2. Never smoke or use a torch in the vicinity of flammable liquids, such as cleaning solvent in open containers.

3. Use the proper sized wrenches to avoid damage to nuts and injury to yourself.

4. When loosening a tight or stuck nut, be guided by what would happen if the wrench should slip. Protect yourself accordingly.

5. Keep your work area clean and uncluttered.

6. Wear safety goggles during all operations involving drilling, grinding, or use of a cold chisel.

7. Never use worn tools.

8. Keep a fire extinguisher handy and be sure it is rated for gasoline and electrical fires.

PARTS REPLACEMENT

Manufacturers make frequent changes during the model year; some relatively major. When you order parts from the dealer or other parts distributor, always order by engine and frame number. Write the numbers down and carry them with you. Compare new parts to the old parts before purchasing them. If they are not alike, have the parts manager explain the difference to you.

EXPENDABLE SUPPLIES

Certain expendable supplies are also required. These include grease, oil, gasket ce-

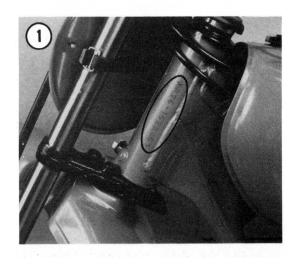

ment, wiping rags, and cleaning solvent. Ask your dealer for the special locking compounds, silicone lubricants, and commercial chain cleaners and lubrication products which make motorcycle maintenance simpler and easier. Solvent is available at most service stations.

SERIAL NUMBERS

You must know the serial number for registration purposes and when ordering parts.

The frame serial number is stamped on the left side of the steering head (**Figure 1**). The engine serial number is stamped on the side of the left crankcase half (**Figure 2**).

CHAPTER TWO

TROUBLESHOOTING

Diagnosing mechanical problems is relatively simple if you use orderly procedures and keep a few basic principles in mind.

The troubleshooting procedures in this chapter analyze typical symptoms and show logical methods of isolating causes. These are not the only methods. There may be several ways to solve a problem, but only a systematic, methodical approach can guarantee success.

Never assume anything. Do not overlook the obvious. If you are riding along and the bike suddenly quits, check the easiest, most accessible problem spots first. Is there gasoline in the tank? Is the fuel shutoff valve in the ON or RESERVE position? Has the spark plug wire fallen off? Check the ignition switch to make sure it is in the RUN position.

If nothing obvious turns up in a quick check, look a little further. Learning to recognize and describe symptoms will make repairs easier for you or a mechanic at the shop. Describe problems accurately and fully. Saying "it won't run" is not the same as saying "it quit on the road at low speed and won't start," or that "it sat in my garage for three months and then wouldn't start."

Gather as many symptoms together as possible to aid in diagnosis. Note whether the engine lost power gradually or all at once, what color smoke (if any) came from the exhaust, and so on. Remember that the more complicated a machine is, the easier it is to troubleshoot because symptoms point to specific problems.

After the symptoms are defined, areas which could cause the problems are tested and analyzed. Guessing at the cause of a problem may provide the solution, but it can easily lead to frustration, wasted time, and a series of expensive, unnecessary parts replacements.

You do not need fancy equipment or complicated test gear to determine whether repairs can be attempted at home. A few simple checks could save a large repair bill and time lost while the bike is in a dealer's service department. On the other hand, be realistic and do not attempt repairs beyond your abilities. Service departments tend to charge heavily for putting together a disassembled engine that may have been abused. Some won't even take on such a job — so use common sense; don't get in over your head.

OPERATING REQUIREMENTS

An engine needs three basics to run properly: correct fuel/air mixture, compression, and a spark at the right time. If one or more of these are missing, the engine won't run. The electrical system is the weakest link of the three basics. More problems result from electrical break-

downs than from any other source. Keep that in mind before you begin tampering with carburetor adjustment and the bike.

If the bike has been sitting for any length of time and refuses to start, check and clean the spark plug and then look to the gasoline delivery system. This includes the tank cap, tank, fuel shutoff valve, lines, and the carburetor. Rust may have formed in the tank, obstructing fuel flow. Gasoline deposits may have gummed up the carburetor jet and air passages. Gasoline tends to lose its potency after standing for long periods. Condensation may contaminate it with water. Drain old gas and try starting with fresh gasoline.

EMERGENCY TROUBLESHOOTING

When the motorcycle is difficult to start or won't start at all, it does not help to continue kicking the pedal down or kick the tires. Check the obvious problems even before getting out your tools. Go down the following list step-by-step. Do each one; you may be embarrassed to find your cutoff switch in the OFF position, but that is better than wearing out your legs trying to get it started. If the bike still won't start, refer to the appropriate troubleshooting procedures which follow in this chapter.

1. Is there fuel in the tank? Remove the filler cap and rock the bike; listen for the fuel sloshing around.

> **WARNING**
> *Do not use an open flame to check in the tank. A serious explosion is certain to result.*

2. Is the fuel shutoff valve (**Figure 1**) in the ON position? Turn it to RESERVE to be sure that you get the last remaining gas.

3. Is the choke in the right position? It should be up for a cold engine (**Figure 2**) and down for a warm engine (**Figure 3**).

4. Is the engine cutoff switch in the ON position (**Figure 4**)?

5. Has the main fuse blown? See Chapter Six for location. Remove it and replace it with one that is known to be good.

ENGINE STARTING PROBLEMS

Check first to see if there is sufficient gas. Open the gas cap and check for gas in the tank by rocking the bike and listening for gas to slosh around. If gas is present in tank, remove the fuel line from the carburetor and see if the gas is flowing through the line. If not, check the fuel shutoff valve to make sure it is in the ON or RESERVE position. If the fuel shutoff valve is in the ON position and still no gas is present, there may be dirt or foreign matter in the fuel line or it may be kinked.

There may also be water in the fuel or the jet in the carburetor may be clogged. Check to see that the area around the neck of the fuel cap is clean and that the fuel shutoff valve is clean. Do not forget to use the choke in trying to start a cold engine. If there is sufficient fuel to the carburetor, check out the electrical system.

Check that the engine cutoff switch is in the RUN position and that the spark plug wire is on tight. If both are OK, remove the spark plug and inspect it; either clean and regap or replace it with a new one. Connect the spark plug wire to the spark plug and lay the spark plug on the cylinder head; make sure that the base of the plug makes good contact. Kick the pedal as though you were trying to start the bike; there should be a big bright blue spark at the tip of the electrode. If there isn't a spark or if the spark is small, then there is an electrical problem.

Check that the spark plug wire is not broken, frayed, or has a loose connection at the spark plug of magneto. If these seem to be in good condition, then check the magneto. The timing may be off, the contacts may be dirty, the condensor worn out or the wire grounded, or the ignition coil may be shorted or open. If any of these problems are evident, refer to Chapter Six for procedures and adjustments.

If there is a good healthy spark and fuel to the carburetor, check to make sure the air cleaner is clean and that the carburetor jet and filter are clean. Make sure that the intake manifold nuts are tight and the carburetor clamp to intake manifold is tight. Check that the gasket between the carburetor and intake manifold is not broken or cracked; replace if necessary.

Check that clutch cable is adjusted properly to engage clutch mechanism when starting.

OPERATING PROBLEMS

Rough Idle

Rough idle is probably caused by incorrect ignition timing or carburetor adjustment, a clogged muffler, or a vacuum leak from loose connections at the carburetor.

Power Loss

The ignition system may have a defective spark plug, ignition coil, or condensor. It is also possible that the timing may be off. The carburetor may be dirty, misadjusted, or it may have the wrong jet size or a dirty air filter. The engine may have worn piston rings, a damaged cylinder, or its valves may need adjustment.

The muffler opening may be clogged by mud or it may need decarbonization. Check also for improper chain tension.

If the engine runs correctly when rear wheel is off of the ground but has no power when riding, check rear wheel bearings for lack of lubrication or damage. Refer to *Rear Wheel and Brake Inspection* in Chapter Seven.

Misfires

This is usually caused by a weak or fouled spark plug, breakdown of the spark plug wire, or a sheared Woodruff key in the magneto. Check to see if a spark "jumps" out from the plug wire to any part of the frame before it gets to the plug. This is best done at night or in a dark garage.

Overheating

This can be caused by too high a spark plug heat range, clogged or dirty cooling fins on the engine cylinder and cylinder head, or incorrect ignition timing. Also check for dragging brakes, a slipping clutch, or a drive chain that needs oil or is adjusted too tightly.

Piston and Engine Seizure

Piston seizure is caused by improper piston to cylinder clearance or broken piston rings. Engine seizure may be caused by a seized piston, broken or seized crankshaft bearings, smashed flywheel magneto cover, buckled magneto or magneto stator screw caught between coil and rotor.

Backfiring

Ignition timing incorrect, engine too cold, a defective spark plug, or contaminated fuel may be the cause of the backfiring.

Engine Noises

Abnormal engine noises are very difficult to describe and diagnose. Knocking may indicate a loose crankshaft assembly caused by bad bearings or a loose or broken engine mounting bolt. Also, the clutch drum may be loose on the crankshaft. A slapping noise usually comes from a loose piston. A slamming noise may be caused by an unrivetted flywheel magneto cam, damaged cylinder caused by overheating, or faulty clutch parts. A rubbing noise may be from the flywheel magneto rotor being bent or out of true, or the cover and rotor touching each other. Pinging is caused by improper ignition timing or too low a gasoline octane rating. If pinging occurs, it should be corrected immediately as it will cause piston damage. A whistling noise may come from loose or damaged bearings, air leaking around the carburetor, or the intake manifold or the magneto breaker cam needing lubrication.

Engine Vibration

Check to see if the engine mounting bolts are loose or broken. Vibration may be caused by worn engine and clutch bearings or an unbalanced rotor in the magneto.

CLUTCH

All clutch troubles except adjustments require partial engine disassembly to identify and cure the problem. See Chapter Five for procedures.

Slippage

This is most noticeable when accelerating in a high gear at relatively low speed. To check slippage, shift to 2nd gear and release the clutch as if riding off. If the clutch is good, the engine will slow and stall. If the clutch slips, continued engine speed will give it away.

Slippage results from insufficient clutch lever free play, worn discs or pressure plate, or weak springs.

Drag or Failure to Release

This trouble usually causes difficult shifting and gear clash, especially when downshifting. The cause may be excessive clutch lever free play, warped or bent pressure plate or clutch disc, broken or loose linings, or lack of lubrication in clutch actuating mechanism.

Chatter or Grabbing

A number of things can cause this trouble. Check tightness of engine mounting bolts. Check for worn or misaligned pressure plate. Also check lever free play.

BRAKES

Loss of braking power is due to worn out linings or improper cable adjustment. If brakes grab, there is probably oil or grease on the linings and they will have to be replaced. If they stick, the return springs may be weak or broken, the pivot cams may need lubrication or the cables need adjusting. Brake grabbing may also be caused by out-of-round drums, broken or glazed brake shoes or no "lead angle" on the leading edges of the brake lining (**Figure 5**). Refer to Chapter Seven.

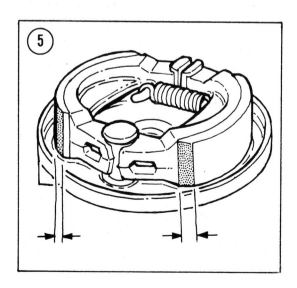

TRANSMISSION

Transmission problems are usually indicated by one or more of the following symptoms:

   a. Difficulty shifting gears

   b. Gear clash when downshifting

   c. Slipping out of gear

   d. Excessive noise in neutral

   e. Excessive noise in gear

Transmission symptoms are sometimes hard to distinguish from clutch symptoms. Be sure that the clutch is not causing the trouble before working on the transmission. Refer to Chapter Five.

SUSPENSION

Hard steering may be caused by improper tire inflation, improper adjustment, or lack of lubrication of the steering head bearings. Wheel shimmy or vibration is caused by misaligned wheels, loose or broken spokes, or worn wheel bearings. Poor handling may be caused by worn shock absorbers, front forks which need lubrication, or a damaged frame and rear swing arm.

CHAPTER THREE

BASIC HAND TOOLS

A number of tools are required to maintain a motorcycle in top condition. You may already have some around for other work such as home and car repairs. There are also tools made especially for motorcycle repairs; these you will have to purchase. In any case, a wide variety of quality tools will make motorcycle repairs more effective and convenient.

Top quality tools are essential — and also more economical. Poor grade tools are made of inferior materials, and are thick, heavy, and clumsy. Their rough finish makes them difficult to clean and they usually don't stand up long.

Quality tools are made of alloy steel and are heat treated for greater strength. They are lighter and better balanced than inferior ones. Their surface is smooth, making them a pleasure to work with and easy to clean. The initial cost of top quality tools may be relatively high, but longer life and ease of use make them less expensive in the long run.

It is aggravating to search for a certain tool in the middle of a repair, only to find it covered with grime. Keep your tools in a tool box. Keep wrench sets, socket sets, etc., together. After using a tool, wipe off dirt and grease with a clean cloth and replace the tool in its correct place.

This chapter describes various hand tools required to perform virtually any repair job on a motorcycle. Each tool is described, and recommendations as to proper size are made for those not familiar with hand tools. **Table 1** includes tools which should be on hand at home for simple repairs or major overhaul.

FASTENERS

In order to better understand and select basic hand tools, a knowledge of various fasteners used on motorcycles is important. This knowledge will also aid in selecting replacements when fasteners are damaged or corroded beyond use.

Threads

Nuts, bolts, and screws are manufactured in a wide range of thread patterns. To join a nut and bolt, it is necessary that the bolt and the diameter of the hole in the nut be the same. It is equally important that the threads on both be properly matched.

The best way to insure that threads on two fasteners are compatible is to turn the nut on the bolt with fingers only. If much force is required, check the thread condition on both fasteners. If thread condition is good, but the fasteners jam, the threads are not compatible. Take the fasteners to a hardware store or motorcycle dealer for proper mates.

Table 1   HOME WORKSHOP TOOLS

Tool	Size or Specifications
Screwdriver	
Slot	$\frac{5}{16}$ x 8 in. blade
Slot	$\frac{3}{8}$ x 12 in. blade
Phillips	Size 2 tip, 6 in. overall
Pliers	
Gas pliers	6 in. overall
Vise Grips	10 in. overall
Needle nose	6 in. overall
Channel lock	12 in. overall
Snap ring	—
Wrenches	
Box-end set	5-14, 22mm
Open-end set	5-14, 22mm
Crescent (adjustable)	6 and 12 in. overall
Socket set	$\frac{1}{2}$ in. drive ratchet with 5-12mm sockets
Spoke wrench	—
Other special tools	
Cable cutter	V-shaped cutting jaws
Impact driver	$\frac{1}{2}$ in. drive with assorted tips
Torque wrench	$\frac{1}{2}$ in. drive—0-100 ft.-lb.
Tire levers	For motorcycle tires

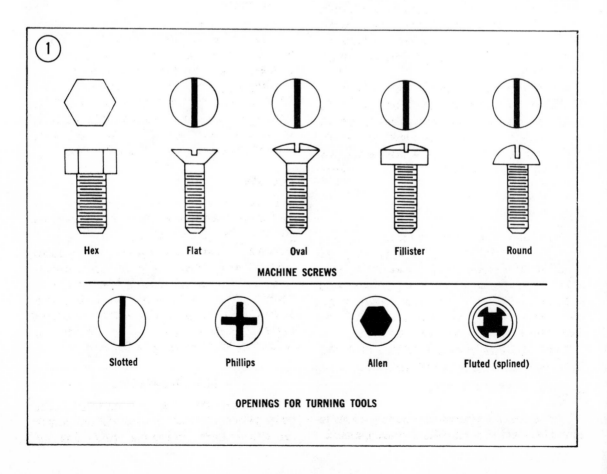

Hex   Flat   Oval   Fillister   Round

MACHINE SCREWS

Slotted   Phillips   Allen   Fluted (splined)

OPENINGS FOR TURNING TOOLS

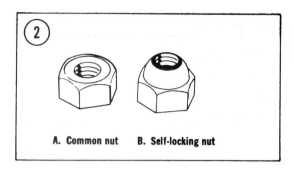

A. Common nut   B. Self-locking nut

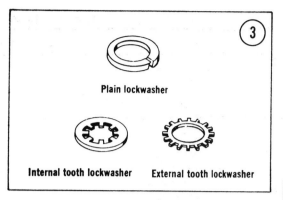

Plain lockwasher

Internal tooth lockwasher   External tooth lockwasher

Most fasteners are cut so that a fastener must be turned clockwise to tighten it. These are called right-hand threads. Some components have left-hand threads; they must be turned counterclockwise to tighten them.

> NOTE: *When replacing threaded components, rely on your dealer's experience; take the old part in for replacement.*

Machine Screws

There are many different types of machine screws. **Figure 1** shows a number of screw heads requiring different types of turning tools. Heads are also designed to protrude above the metal (round) or to be slightly recessed in the metal (flat).

When replacing a damaged screw, take it to a hardware store or motorcycle dealer. Match the head type, diameter, and threads exactly. In addition, match the type of metal used. For example, if the old screw is chrome plated, the new one must be chrome plated also to resist corrosion and rust.

Bolts

Commonly called bolts, the technical name for these fasteners is cap screws. They are specified by diameter and thread pitch, e.g., M14 x 1 specifies a bolt 14mm in diameter with a thread pitch of 1mm. The measurement across two flats on the head of the bolt indicates the proper wrench size to be used.

When replacing damaged bolts, follow the same advice given for machine screws.

Nuts

Nuts are manufactured in a variety of types and sizes. Most nuts on bikes are hexagonal (6-

sided) and fit on bolts, screws, and studs with the same diameter and threads-per-inch.

Figure 2 shows several nuts usually found on bikes. The common nut (A), is normally used with a lockwasher. The nut (B) has a nylon insert which prevents the nut from loosening and does not require a locknut. To indicate the size of the nut, manufacturers specify the diameter of the opening and the thread pitch, e.g., M14 x 1 indicates a 14mm opening and a 1mm thread pitch.

This is, of course, the same as for bolts, but with no length dimension given. In addition, the measurement across two flats on the nut indicates the proper wrench size to be used.

When replacing a damaged nut, take it to a hardware store or motorcycle dealer. Match the type, diameter, and threads exactly. In addition, match the type of metal used, e.g., chrome plating to resist rust and corrosion.

Washers

There are two major types of washers — flat washers and lockwashers. Flat washers are simple discs with a hole to fit a screw or bolt. Lockwashers are designed to prevent a fastener from working loose, due to vibration, expansion, and contraction. **Figure 3** shows several washers. Note that flat washers are often used between a lockwasher and a fastener to act as a smooth bearing surface. This permits the fastener to be turned easily with a tool.

SCREWDRIVERS

The screwdriver is a very basic tool, but many people don't use it properly and consequently, do more damage than good. The slot

3

on a screw has a definite dimension and shape. A screwdriver must be selected to conform to that shape. A small screwdriver in a large slot will twist the screwdriver out of shape and damage the slot. A large screwdriver on a small slot will also damage the slot. In addition, since the sides of the screw slot are parallel, the sides of the screwdriver near the tip must be parallel. If tip sides are tapered, the screwdriver wedges itself out of the slot; this makes the screw difficult to remove and may damage the slot.

Two basic types of screwdrivers are required to repair the motorcycle — a common screwdriver and a Phillips screwdriver. Both types are illustrated in **Figure 4**.

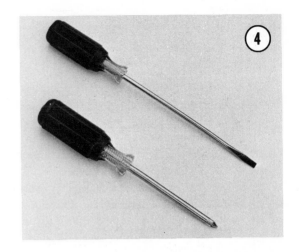

Screwdrivers are available in sets which often include an assortment of common and Phillips blades. If you purchase individual screwdrivers, as a minimum obtain:

a. Common screwdriver, $\frac{5}{16}$ x 6 in. blade
b. Common screwdriver, $\frac{3}{8}$ x 12 in. blade
c. Phillips screwdriver, size 2, 6 in. blade

Use screwdrivers only for driving screws. Never use a screwdriver for prying or chiseling. In addition, never use a common screwdriver to remove a Phillips or Allen head screw; you can damage the head so that even the proper tool cannot remove the screw.

Keep screwdrivers in proper condition and they will last longer and perform better. Always keep the tip in good condition. **Figure 5** shows how to grind the tip to proper shape if it is damaged. Note the parallel sides at the tip.

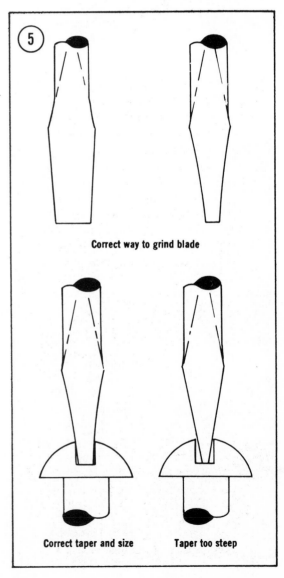

Correct way to grind blade

Correct taper and size   Taper too steep

PLIERS

Pliers come in a wide range of types and sizes. Pliers are useful for cutting, bending, and crimping. They should never be used to cut hardened objects or to turn nuts or bolts. **Figure 6** shows several pliers useful in motorcycle repairs.

Each type of pliers has a specialized function. Gas pliers are general purpose and are used mainly for holding things and bending. Vise Grips are used as pliers or to grip objects very tightly like a vise. Needle nose pliers are used to hold or bend small objects. Channel lock pliers can be adjusted to hold various size objects; the jaws remain parallel to grip round objects such

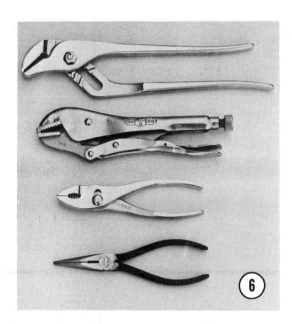

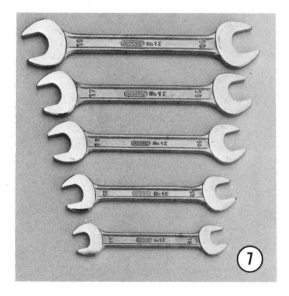

as pipe or tubing. There are many more types of pliers. The ones described here are most suitable for motorcycle repairs.

BOX AND OPEN-END WRENCHES

Box wrenches and open-end wrenches are available in sets or separately in a variety of sizes. See **Figures 7 and 8**. The size stamped near the end refers to the distance between two parallel flats on a hex head bolt or nut.

A set covering 5-14mm and 22mm is adequate for service on the motorcycle.

Box wrenches are usually superior to open-end wrenches. Open-end wrenches grip a nut on only two flats. Unless it fits well, it may slip and round off the points on the nut. The box wrench grips all six flats. Both 6-point and 12-point openings on box wrenches are available. The 6-point gives superior holding power; the 12-point allows a shorter swing.

Combination wrenches which are open on one end and boxed on the other are also available. Both ends are the same size.

ADJUSTABLE (CRESCENT) WRENCHES

An adjustable wrench (also called crescent wrench) can be adjusted to fit nearly any nut or bolt head. See **Figure 9**. However, it can loosen and slip, causing damage to the nut. Use only when other wrenches are not available.

Crescent wrenches come in sizes ranging from 4-18 in. overall. A 6 or 8 in. wrench is recommended as an all-purpose wrench.

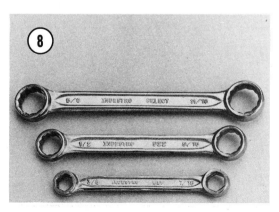

SOCKET WRENCHES

This type is undoubtedly the fastest, safest, and most convenient to use. See **Figure 10**. Sockets which attach to a ratchet handle are available with 6-point or 12-point openings and $\frac{1}{4}$, $\frac{3}{8}$, $\frac{1}{2}$, and $\frac{3}{4}$ inch drives. The drive size indicates the size of the square hole which mates with the ratchet handle. Sockets are available in metric and inch sizes.

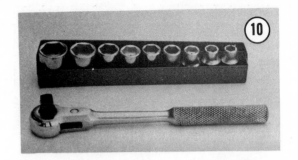

STRAP WRENCH

This tool is used for holding the magneto rotor to keep it from turning while removing the nut. See **Figure 11**.

TORQUE WRENCH

A torque wrench is used with a socket to measure how tight a nut or bolt is installed. See **Figure 12**. They come in a wide price range and with either $\frac{3}{8}$ or $\frac{1}{2}$ in. square drive. The drive size indicates the size of the square drive which mates with the socket. An inexpensive one that measures from 1-100 ft.-lb. (0-140 N•m) retails for about $15.

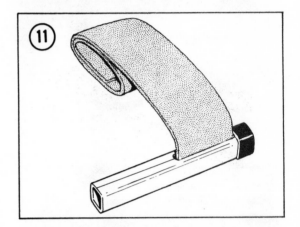

IMPACT DRIVER

This tool might have been designed with the motorcycle in mind. See **Figure 13**. It makes removal of engine and clutch parts easy and eliminates damage to bolts and screw slots. A good one runs about $15 at large hardware or auto parts stores.

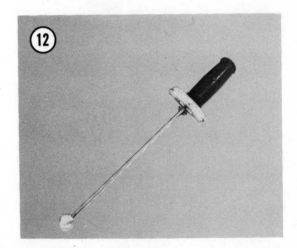

IGNITION GAUGE

This tool measures point gap. It also has round wire gauges for measuring spark plug gap. See **Figure 14**. A good one runs about $3 and is available at most auto or motorcycle supply stores.

TIRE LEVER

These are used to remove or install motorcycle tires. See **Figure 15**. Check the working end of the tool before use and remove any burrs. Never use a screwdriver in place of a tire lever. Chapter Seven explains its use.

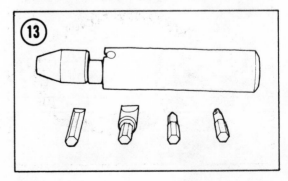

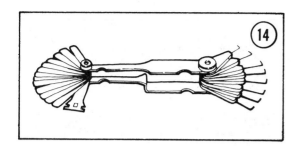

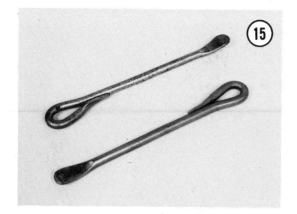

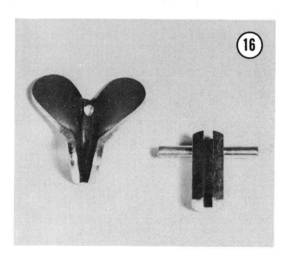

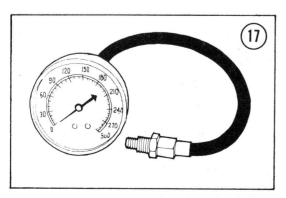

SPOKE WRENCH

This special wrench is used to tighten spokes (**Figure 16**). It is available at most motorcycle supply shops.

TUNE-UP AND TROUBLESHOOTING TOOLS

Engine tune-up and troubleshooting procedures require a few more tools, described in the following sections.

Compression Gauge

An engine with low compression cannot be properly tuned and will not develop full power. A compression gauge measures engine compression. The one shown in **Figure 17** has a flexible stem which enables it to reach cylinders where there is little clearance between the cylinder head and frame. This is not necessary on the XR75. Inexpensive ones start around $3, available at auto accessory stores or by mail order from large catalog order firms.

Dwell Meter

A dwell meter measures the distance in degrees of cam rotation that the breaker points remain closed while the engine is running. Since this angle is determined by breaker point gap, dwell angle is an accurate indication of breaker point gap.

Many tachometers intended for tuning and testing incorporate a dwell meter as well. See **Figure 18**. Follow the manufacturer's instructions to measure dwell.

Tachometer

A tachometer is necessary for tuning. Ignition timing and carburetor adjustments must be performed at the specified idle speed. The best instrument for this purpose is one with a low range of 0-1,000 or 0-2,000 rpm for setting idle, and a high range of 0-4,000 or more for setting ignition timing at 3,000 rpm. Extended range (0-6,000 or 0-8,000) instruments lack accuracy at lower speeds. The instrument should be capable of detecting changes of 25 rpm on the low range.

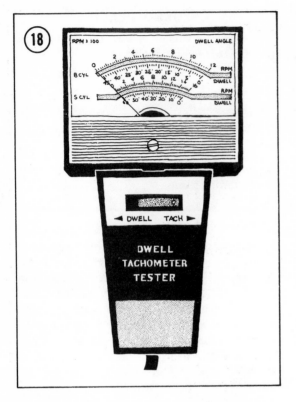

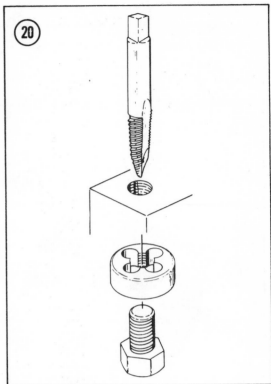

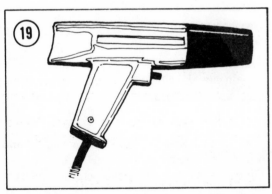

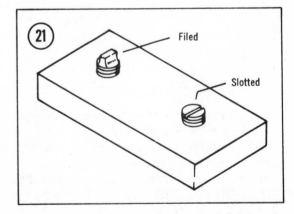

Strobe Timing Light

This instrument is necessary for tuning. It permits very accurate ignition timing. By flashing a light at the precise instant that the cylinder fires, the position of the flywheel at that instant can be seen. Marks on the flywheel are lined up with the transmission case mark while the engine is running.

Suitable lights range from inexpensive neon bulb types ($2-$3) to powerful xenon strobe lights ($20-$40). See **Figure 19**. Neon timing lights are difficult to see and must be used in dimly lit areas. Xenon strobe timing lights can be used outside in bright sunlight. Both types work on this motorcycle; use according to the manufacturer's instructions.

MECHANIC'S TIPS

Removing Frozen Nuts and Screws

When a fastener rusts and can't be removed, several methods may be used to loosen it. First, apply penetrating oil such as Liquid Wrench or WD-40 (available at any hardware or auto supply store). Apply it liberally. Rap the fastener

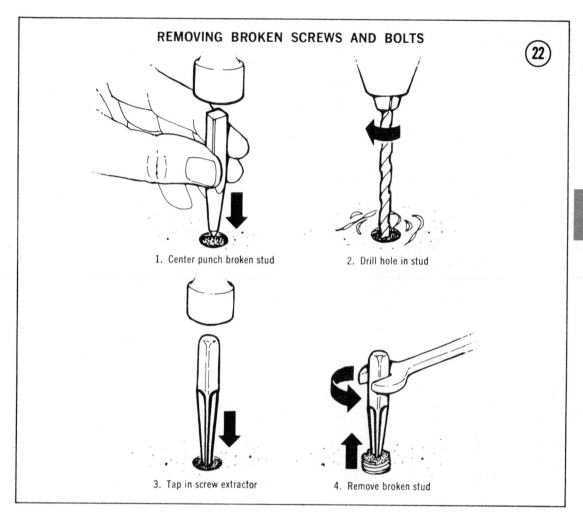

REMOVING BROKEN SCREWS AND BOLTS

(22)

1. Center punch broken stud

2. Drill hole in stud

3. Tap in screw extractor

4. Remove broken stud

3

several times with a small hammer; don't hit it hard enough to cause damage.

For frozen screws, apply oil as described, then insert a screwdriver in the slot and rap the top of the screwdriver with a hammer. This loosens the rust so the screw can be removed in the normal way. If the screw head is too chewed up to use a screwdriver, grip the head with Vise Grip pliers and twist the screw out.

For a frozen bolt or nut, apply penetrating oil, then rap it with a hammer. Remove with a proper size wrench. If the points are rounded off, grip with Vise Grip as described for screws.

Remedying Stripped Threads

Occasionally, threads are stripped through carelessness or impact damage. Often the threads can be cleaned up by running a tap (for

internal threads on nuts) or die (for external threads on bolts) through the threads. See **Figure 20**.

Removing Broken Screws or Bolts

When the head breaks off a screw or bolt, several methods are available for removing the remaining portion.

If a large portion of the remainder projects out, try gripping it with Vise Grips. If the projecting portion is too small, try filing it to fit a wrench or cut a slot in it to fit a screwdriver **(Figure 21)**.

If the head breaks off flush, try using a screw extractor. To do this, center punch the exact center of the remaining portion of the screw or bolt. Drill a small hole in the screw and tap the extractor into the hole. Back the screw out with a wrench on the extractor. See **Figure 22**.

CHAPTER FOUR

TUNE-UP, LUBRICATION, AND MAINTENANCE

If this is your first experience with an engine-powered vehicle, you should become acquainted with products that are available in auto or motorcycle parts and supply stores. Look into the tune-up tools and parts; check out the different lubricants, motor oil, chain cleaner, chain oil, and greases. Also check engine degreaser, like Gunk Cycle Degreaser, for cleaning your bike prior to working on it. See what is available to maintain the appearance properly, such as polish and wax for the painted surfaces, Armor All for rubber and vinyl, and Simichrome for all plated, polished, and stainless parts.

The more you get involved with your bike, the more you will want to work on it. Start out by doing the simple tune-up, lubrication, and maintenance. Tackle more involved jobs as you gain experience so that you will not get frustrated and discouraged.

The Honda XR75 is a relatively simple machine but it does require periodic attention to keep it working properly. Without proper attention, you may soon face a number of expensive repairs.

Most expensive repairs can be prevented. A regular program of periodic inspection, lubrication, and maintenance will help find trouble before it becomes major and actually prevent most trouble due to wear.

This chapter explains tune-up, periodic adjustments, maintenance, inspection, and lubrication required for the XR75.

You can perform all of the procedures in less than one day. Considering the number of carefree, safe, and enjoyable hours of riding possible with a well-maintained bike, maintenance time represents a "bargain" investment.

ENGINE TUNE-UP

The number of definitions of the term "tune-up" is probably equal to the number of people defining it. For purposes of this book, a tune-up is general adjustment and maintenance to ensure peak engine power.

The following paragraphs discuss each facet of a proper tune-up which should be performed in the order given. Unless otherwise specified, the engine should be thoroughly cool before starting any tune-up service.

The engine tune-up should be performed every six months.

Cylinder Head Nuts

1. Remove the seat and the fuel tank.

2. Remove the 2 bolts (3 acorn nuts on 1975-1976 models), securing the cylinder head cover and remove it.

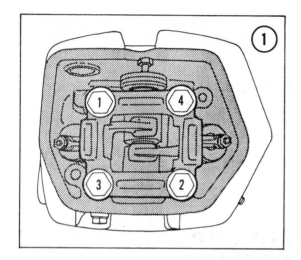

3. Tighten the nuts in the sequence shown in **Figure 1**. Torque the nuts to 5.8-8.7 ft.-lb. (8-12 N•m).

The fuel tank seat and cylinder head cover should be left off at this time for the following procedure.

Valve Clearance Adjustment

Valve clearance adjustment must be made with the engine cold. The correct clearance of both the intake and exhaust valves is 0.002 in. (0.05mm).

1. Remove the 5 screws securing the left-hand engine cover and remove it.

2. Rotate the crankshaft with the kickstarter until the piston is at top dead center (TDC) on the compression stroke. A cylinder at TDC will have both its rocker arms loose, indicating that the exhaust valve and the intake valve are closed.

3. Make sure that the "T" on the flywheel aligns with the pointer. See **Figure 2** for 1975-1976 models and **Figure 3** for 1977 and later models.

4. Check the clearance of both valves by inserting a flat feeler gauge between the adjusting screw and the valve stem (**Figure 4**). When the clearance is correct, there will be a slight resistance on the feeler gauge when it is inserted and withdrawn.

5. To correct the clearance, back off the locknut and screw the adjuster either in or out to correct the clearance, until a slight resistance can be felt on the gauge. Hold the adjuster to prevent it from turning further, and tighten the

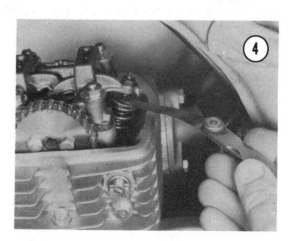

locknut. Then, recheck the clearance to make sure the adjuster did not turn after the correct clearance was achieved.

6. Install the left-hand engine cover, cylinder head cover, seat, and fuel tank.

Compression Test

At every tune-up, check cylinder compression. Record the results and compare them at the next tune-up. A running record will show trends in deterioration so that corrective action can be taken before complete failure.

The results, when properly interpreted, can indicate general cylinder, piston ring, and valve condition.

1. Warm the engine to normal operating temperature. Ensure that the choke valve and throttle valve are completely open.

2. Remove the spark plug.

3. Connect the compression tester to the cylinder following manufacturer's instructions.

4. Have an assistant crank the engine over until there is no further rise in pressure.

5. Remove the tester and record the reading.

The reading should be 171 + 13 psi (12 + 1 kg^2). A greater difference indicates worn or broken rings, leaky or sticky valves, blown head gasket, or a combination of all.

If the reading is within the above specified amount, rings and valves are in good condition.

If a low reading, below 155 psi (10.8 kg^2), is obtained on the cylinder, it indicates valve or ring trouble. To determine which, pour about a teaspoon of engine oil through the spark plug hole onto the top of the piston. Turn the engine over once to clear some of the excess oil, then take another compression test and record the reading. If the compression returns to normal, the valves are good but the rings are defective. If compression does not increase, the valves require servicing. A valve could be hanging open, but not burned, or a piece of carbon could be on a valve seat.

Spark Plug

Every 30 operating days, or sooner if necessary, remove the spark plug. To remove the spark plug, first clean the area around its base to prevent dirt or other material from entering the cylinder. Next, remove the spark plug wire from the top of the spark plug by pulling straight off. Unscrew the spark plug, using the spark plug wrench or use a $^{13}\!/_{16}$ in. deep socket wrench. If difficulty is encountered removing the spark plug, apply penetrating oil, like Liquid Wrench or WD-40, to its base and allow about 20 minutes for the oil to work in.

After removing the spark plug, check its condition with those shown in **Figure 5**. If it has a light tan or gray-colored deposit and no abnormal gap wear or electrode erosion is evident, the engine is running properly. Clean the end that goes into the cylinder head with a wire brush. Inspect it for a worn or eroded electrode. These are the two points which the spark jumps (**Figure 6**). Replace the spark plug if there is any doubt about its condition. If the spark plug is OK, file the center electrode square, then adjust the gap by bending the outer electrode only with a spark plug gapper tool (**Figure 7**). Measure the gap with a round wire spark plug gauge as shown in **Figure 8**. Do not use a flat gauge as it will indicate an incorrect reading. The proper gap should be between 0.024-0.028 in. (0.6-0.7mm).

Before installing the spark plug, clean the seating area on the cylinder head and always use a new gasket. Install the plug only finger-tight, then tighten it an additional one-half turn with a spark plug wrench. Wipe off top tip of the spark plug and install spark plug wire.

It is a good idea to carry a spare spark plug with you at all times. Keep it in its original package to protect it.

The proper spark plug is — NGK C-7HS or ND U22FS.

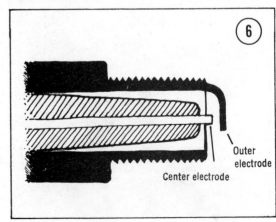

Outer electrode

Center electrode

⑤ SPARK PLUG CONDITION

NORMAL
• Identified by light tan or gray deposits on the firing tip.
• Can be cleaned.

GAP BRIDGED
• Identified by deposit buildup closing gap between electrodes.
• Caused by oil or carbon fouling. If deposits are not excessive, the plug can be cleaned.

OIL FOULED
• Identified by wet black deposits on the insulator shell bore electrodes.
• Caused by excessive oil entering combustion chamber through worn rings and pistons, excessive clearance between valve guides and stems, or worn or loose bearings. Can be cleaned. If engine is not repaired, use a hotter plug.

CARBON FOULED
• Identified by black, dry fluffy carbon deposits on insulator tips, exposed shell surfaces and electrodes.
• Caused by too cold a plug, weak ignition, dirty air cleaner, too rich a fuel mixture, or excessive idling. Can be cleaned.

LEAD FOULED
• Identified by dark gray, black, yellow, or tan deposits or a fused glazed coating on the insulator tip.
• Caused by highly leaded gasoline. Can be cleaned.

WORN
• Identified by severely eroded or worn electrodes.
• Caused by normal wear. Should be replaced.

FUSED SPOT DEPOSIT
• Identified by melted or spotty deposits resembling bubbles or blisters.
• Caused by sudden acceleration. Can be cleaned.

OVERHEATING
• Identified by a white or light gray insulator with small black or gray brown spots and with bluish-burnt appearance of electrodes.
• Caused by engine overheating, wrong type of fuel, loose spark plugs, too hot a plug, or incorrect ignition timing. Replace the plug.

PREIGNITION
• Identified by melted electrodes and possibly blistered insulator. Metallic deposits on insulator indicate engine damage.
• Caused by wrong type of fuel, incorrect ignition timing or advance, too hot a plug, burned valves, or engine overheating. Replace the plug.

4

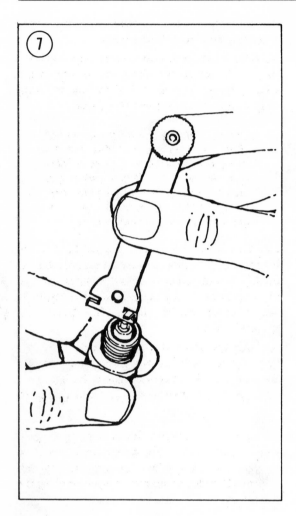

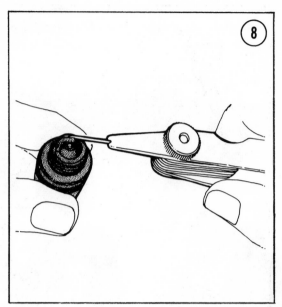

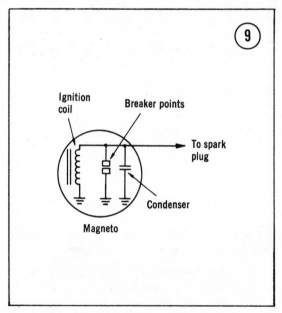

Ignition coil

Breaker points

To spark plug

Condenser

Magneto

Magneto

The engine-mounted magneto generates electricity for the spark plug. It works similar to a generator or alternator on an automobile, but is more compact and is attached directly to the engine.

The stator is stationary and consists of a coil of specially wound wire attached to the engine crankcase. The rotor has built-in permanent magnets which rotate with the engine crankshaft. As the magnets move past the stationary coils, they induce a voltage within these coils which powers the spark plug.

The ignition breaker points, in the magneto, are used to regulate current flow from the ignition coil to the spark plug, at just the right time, when the piston reaches firing position. When the breaker points are closed, the current is grounded — thus, no current to the spark plug.

When they open, the current that has built up in the coil is no longer grounded and is allowed to flow from the coil directly to the spark plug, bypassing the breaker points. This sudden burst of current jumps the spark plug gap, creating the spark for igniting the fuel mixture. To prevent the points from arcing when they open, a condenser is placed in the circuit.

Figure 9 illustrates the breaker points and condenser in the ignition circuit leading to the spark plug.

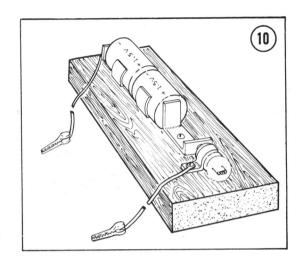

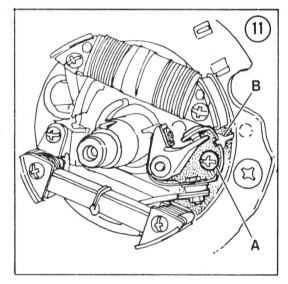

3. Disconnect the primary electrical wire (black/white) from the magneto.

4. Rotate the rotor counterclockwise until the mark "F" aligns with the mark on the crankcase (**Figure 3**). On 1975-1976 models, the pointer is on the side cover (**Figure 2**).

> NOTE: *Prior to attaching the tester, check the condition of the batteries by touching the two test leads together. The light should be* ON. *If not, replace the batteries and/or check all connections on the tester. Be sure the tester is operating correctly before using it.*

5. Connect one test lead of the test light to the black/white magneto wire disconnected in Step 3, and the other to a good ground like one of the cooling fins of the cylinder. The test light should be on, but should be dim. The points should be open.

6. Turn the rotor clockwise a little. The test light should now brighten; the points should now be closed indicating proper timing. If it does not, the contact points must be adjusted to provide proper timing.

7. Loosen the contact breaker point attachment screw (A, **Figure 11**) and insert a screwdriver between the adjusting notches (B, **Figure 11**) and turn slightly to open or close the point gap.

> NOTE: *Opening the point gap will advance the timing (the spark plug will fire sooner) and closing the gap will retard it (the spark plug will fire later).*

> NOTE: *Figure 11 is shown with the magneto rotor removed for clarity. Do not remove it to perform this adjustment procedure.*

8. After adjusting, tighten the attachment screw (A, **Figure 11**) and recheck the timing by repeating Steps 5 and 6. If necessary, repeat Step 7 until the timing is correct.

9. After the timing is correct, see that the contact breaker point gap is within 0.012-0.016 in. (0.3-0.4mm). If the gap exceeds these dimensions, the contact point assembly should be replaced as described under *Contact Breaker Point Replacement* in this chapter.

Breaker Point Adjustment and Magneto Timing

This procedure requires a test light. It can be a homemade unit (**Figure 10**) that consists of two C or D size flashlight batteries and a light bulb, all mounted on a piece of wood, some light gauge electrical wire and alligator clips. These items can be purchased from any hardware store.

The following procedure is based on the test unit shown in **Figure 10**. If another type is used, follow the manufacturer's instructions.

1. Remove the 6 screws securing the left-hand engine cover and remove it.

2. Turn the engine cutoff switch to the RUN position.

Breaker Points Inspection and Cleaning

Through normal use, the surfaces of the breaker points gradually pit and burn. If they are not too badly pitted, they can be dressed with a few strokes of a clean point file or Flexstone (available at most auto parts stores). Do not use emery cloth or sandpaper, as particles remain on the points and cause arcing and burning. If a few strokes of the file do not smooth the points completely, replace them.

If points are still serviceable after filing, remove all residue with lacquer thinner. Close the points on a piece of clean white paper such as a business card. Continue to pull the card through the closed points until no particles or discoloration are transferred to the card. Finally, rotate the engine and observe the points as they open and close. If they do not meet squarely (**Figure 12**) replace them as described under *Contact Breaker Point Replacement* in this chapter.

Contact Breaker Point Replacement

1. Remove the 5 screws securing the left-hand engine cover and remove it.

2. Remove the nut securing the rotor to the crankshaft.

> NOTE: *To prevent the rotor from turning, hold it with a strap wrench (Figure 13) or a special tool (Figure 14).*

3. Remove the rotor with a flywheel puller (Honda part No. 07016-00102). See **Figure 15**. The flywheel puller has left-hand threads so it must be installed counterclockwise. Screw the outer body in until it stops. Hold the outer body stationary with a wrench and turn the inner body until the rotor disengages from the crankshaft. Remove the rotor.

4. Remove the nut (A, **Figure 16**) attaching the electrical terminal and attachment screw (B, **Figure 16**) securing the contact breaker point assembly to the stator.

5. Install by reversing the removal steps; tighten rotor nut to 22-28 ft.-lb. (30-38 N•m).

6. Adjust the timing as described under *Breaker Point Adjustment and Magneto Timing* in this chapter.

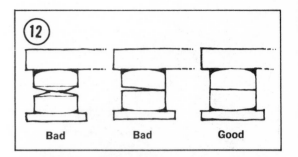
Bad   Bad   Good

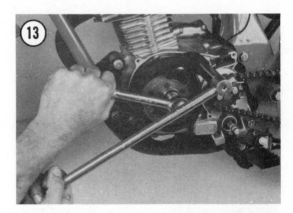

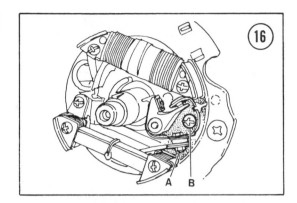

Air Filter

The air filter element traps dirt and dust and keeps it from the engine. It must be kept clean or it will restrict the air intake for the engine, thus reducing engine performance. It should be cleaned every 30 operating days or every three months, whichever comes first.

1. Remove the right-hand side number plate.

2. Remove the 3 nuts securing the air filter cover (**Figure 17**) and remove it.

3. Remove the air filter element (**Figure 18**) and thoroughly wash it in cleaning solvent. Squeeze out all remaining solvent and let it air dry.

4. Soak the element in SAE 80 or 90 clean gear oil or special filter oil. Squeeze out all excess oil as it will restrict air flow.

5. Reassemble the element onto the air filter (**Figure 19**) and reinstall.

Carburetor Adjustment

Idle speed should be set to 1,400 rpm. If a tachometer is not available, set the idle to the lowest speed that allows the engine to continue running at all times. Even when hot, the engine should idle once the clutch is disengaged and the transmission placed in neutral.

The engine should be at normal operating temperature prior to adjusting the carburetor.

1. Set the idle speed to 1,400 rpm with the idle speed screw (A, **Figure 20**).

2. Screw the idle mixture screw (B, **Figure 20**) carefully in until it seats. Back the screw out 1¼ turns.

CAUTION
Do not screw the idle mixture screw in tight or the seat in the carburetor will be damaged.

3. Turn the idle mixture screw counterclockwise until the engine misses or idle speed decreases. Note the position of the screw.

4. Turn the idle mixture screw clockwise until the engine misses or idle speed decreases. Note the position of the screws.

5. Set the idle mixture screw midway between the 2 points.

6. Readjust the idle speed to 1,400 rpm.

LUBRICANTS

Oil

Oil is graded according to its viscosity, which is an indication of how thick it is. The Society of Automotive Engineers (SAE) system distinguishes oil viscosity by numbers, called "weights." Thick (heavy) oils have higher viscosity numbers than thin (light) oils, for example, a 5-weight (SAE 5) oil is a light oil while a 90-weight (SAE 90) oil is relatively heavy. The viscosity of an oil has nothing to do with its lubricating properties.

In this manual, many procedures specify light oil. This means an SAE 5 oil or equivalent.

Grease

Molybdenum disulphide grease is preferable as a lubricant for many parts of a motorcycle. Water does not wash grease off parts as easily as it washes off oil. In addition, grease maintains its lubricating qualities better than oil on long rides. In a pinch, though, the wrong lubricant is better than none at all. Correct the situation as soon as possible.

A number of procedures in this manual specify thin grease. Lubri-Plate, a white grease, is highly satisfactory for a motorcycle and comes in a small tube for easy application.

CLEANING SOLVENTS

A number of solvents can be used to remove old dirt, grease, and oil. Kerosene is readily available and comparatively inexpensive. Another inexpensive solvent similar to kerosene is ordinary diesel fuel. Both of these solvents have very high temperature flash point and can be used safely in any adequately ventilated area away from open flames.

WARNING
Never use gasoline. Gasoline is extremely volatile and contains tremendously destructive potential energy. The slightest spark from metal parts accidentally hitting or a tool slipping could cause a fatal explosion.

ROUTINE CHECKS

Engine Oil Level

The engine dipstick is located on the right side just behind the kickstarter lever (**Figure 21**). Place the motorcycle on level ground, hold it upright and unscrew the dipstick. The level should be checked with dipstick inserted in the hole but not screwed in. Oil level should be up to the upper level on the gauge (**Figure 22**). The recommended oils are:

   SAE 10W-40 for all seasons
   SAE 20W-50 for temperatures above
      60°F (15°C)

General Inspection

1. Examine the engine for signs of oil leakage.

2. Check for loose spokes in both wheels.

3. Check the drive chain for lubrication and proper tension. Chain free play should be ¼ in. (20mm). See **Figure 23**. Refer to *Drive Chain Adjustment* in this chapter.

4. Check for loose bolts and nuts.

5. Check front and rear shocks for signs of oil leaks. See Chapter Eight, *Frame and Suspension,* for repair.

Tire Pressure

Tire pressure must be checked with the tires cold. A simple, accurate gauge (**Figure 24**) can be purchased for a few dollars and should be carried in your motorcycle tool kit.

The correct tire pressure is:
   Front tire — 17 psi (1.2 kg²)
   Rear tire — 20 psi (1.4 kg²)

4

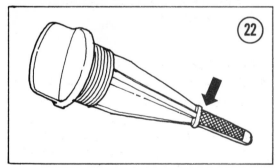

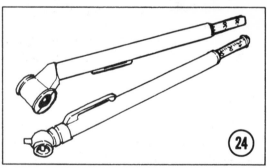

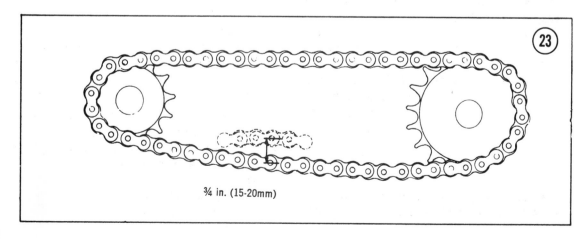

¾ in. (15-20mm)

Tire Inspection

Check the tread for excessive wear, deep cuts, imbedded objects such as stones, nails, glass, etc. If you find a nail in a tire, mark its location with a light crayon before pulling it out. This will help locate the hole in the inner tube. Refer to *Tire Changing* in Chapter Seven.

PERIODIC LUBRICATION

Changing Engine Oil

The factory recommends oil change intervals of 30 operating days or every three months, whichever comes first. This assumes that the motorcycle is operated in moderate climates. In extremely cold climates, oil should be changed every 30 days. The time interval is more important than the mileage interval because acids formed by gasoline and water vapor from combustion will contaminate the oil even if the motorcycle is not run for several months. Also, if the motorcycle is operated under extremely dusty conditions, as the XR75 will most likely be used, the oil will get dirty more quickly and should be changed more frequently than recommended.

Use only a detergent oil with a API rating of SE or better. The quality rating is stamped on the top of the can. Try to use the same brand of oil every time. Oil additives are not recommended.

1. Start the engine and run it until it is at normal operating temperature, then shut it off.

2. Place a drip pan under the crankcase and remove the drain plug (**Figure 25**). Remove the dipstick; this will speed up the flow of oil.

3. Let it drain for at least 15-20 minutes, during which time, kick the kickstarter a couple of times to help drain any remaining oil.

CAUTION
Make sure that the ignition switch is in the OFF *position.*

4. Inspect the sealing washer on the drain plug, replace if necessary. Install the drain plug.

5. Fill the crankcase with approximately 0.9 quart (1.0 liter) of the recommended weight oil. Install the dipstick.

    SAE 10W-40 for all seasons
    SAE 20W-50 for temperatures
      above 60°F (15°C)

6. Start the engine and let it run at idle speed; check for oil leaks.

7. Turn off the engine and check for correct oil level. Add oil if necessary to maintain the oil level up to the upper mark on the dipstick (**Figure 22**).

Wheel Bearings

The wheel bearings should be cleaned and repacked every year or after crossing or riding in small rivers or creeks. The correct service procedure is covered in Chapter Seven.

Front and Rear Brake Cams

Every year, remove the front and rear wheels, remove the brake backing plate assemblies and lubricate the pivot pins and cams as described in Chapter Seven.

Cables

Every 30 operating days or three months, whichever comes first, squirt a few drops of light oil in the brake and clutch lever cables where they enter the cable housing at the hand levers (**Figure 26**).

Drive Chain

Every 30 operating days or three months, whichever comes first, remove the chain, then clean and lubricate it as described in Chapter Seven.

Steering Head Bearings

Every year, remove the upper and lower steering head bearings. Clean, inspect and lubricate them as described in Chapter Eight.

Front Forks — Changing Oil

The oil in the front forks should be changed every year. The recommended type and quantity of oil is essential for good handling.

1. Remove the drain plug (**Figure 27**) at the base of each fork leg and drain the oil into a drip pan. *Do not reuse the oil.*

2. Install the drain plugs and remove the two front fork top bolts. See **Figure 28**.

3. Fill each fork leg with 3.7 oz. (110cc) of ATF (Automatic Transmission Fluid).

NOTE: *In order to measure the correct amount of oil, use a plastic baby bottle.*

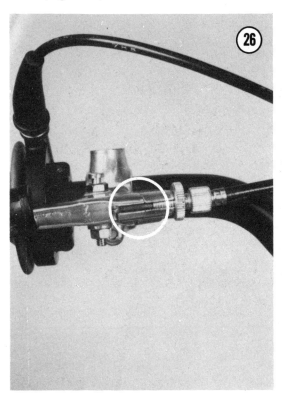

These have measured increments in fluid ounces (oz.) and cubic centimeters (cc) on the side (Figure 29).

4. Install the front fork top bolts.

PERIODIC MAINTENANCE

The following service should be performed every 30 operating days or every three months, whichever comes first.

Throttle Operation

The throttle twistgrip and the cable are susceptible to dirt and water and should be checked and adjusted periodically. Just how often will depend on the usage and the area in which the machine is used. Refer to **Table 1**.

1. Loosen the 2 screws securing the throttle assembly to the handlebar and remove the throttle **(Figure 30)**.

2. Disassemble the throttle housing and clean all the parts thoroughly.

3. Grease the twistgrip and twistgrip housing; check the cable end for wear or frayed wire.

4. Check the cable for freedom of movement. If there are tight spots or the cable is difficult to operate, replace it.

5. Clean the end of the handlebar and apply a thin coat of grease.

6. Reassemble the throttle assembly on the handlebar and connect the cable.

Table 1   SERVICE INTERVALS

With each tank of gas
- Check engine oil level.
- Check tire pressure.
- Check, adjust, and lube drive chain.

Every 30 operating days or 3 months
- Check throttle operation.
  Make adjustments as required.
- Inspect/clean fuel lines.
- Check/adjust clutch.
- Check/adjust brakes.
- Check tires.
- Inspect/clean air filter.
- Change engine oil.
- Inspect/adjust rims and spokes.
- Check/adjust suspension components.
- Check all fasteners. Tighten where required.
- Check/adjust valve clearance.
- Inspect/clean spark plug.
- Check/adjust breaker points.
- Check/adjust ignition timing.

Every year
- Replace spark plug.
- Replace air filter.
- Lubricate steering head bearings.
- Check/adjust cam chain.
- Change fork oil.

Clutch Adjustment

For proper clutch operation, the clutch adjusting lever, located within the right-hand engine cover, must be adjusted first and then the free play of the clutch cable should be adjusted.

The clutch cable can be adjusted at both ends. Normal adjustment can be made by means of the lower cable adjuster, located on the right-hand engine cover, and fine adjustment using the upper adjuster on the clutch lever on the handlebar.

The clutch lever free play should be between 0.4-0.8 in. (10-20mm). See **Figure 31**.

Clutch Adjusting Lever

Loosen the clutch adjuster locknut (A, **Figure 32**) and turn the clutch adjuster (B, **Figure 32**) counterclockwise until it stops. Then turn the clutch adjuster (B) back ⅛-¼ turn and tighten the locknut.

Clutch Cable Lower Adjuster

Loosen the locknut (A, **Figure 33**) and turn the adjuster (B, **Figure 33**) clockwise to decrease free play. After the correct amount of free play is achieved, tighten the locknut and check that the clutch operates properly.

4

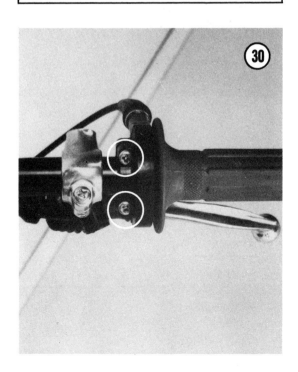

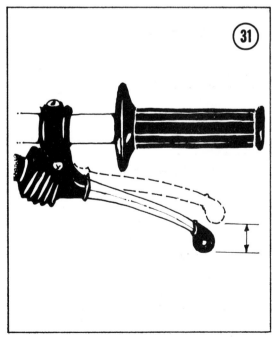

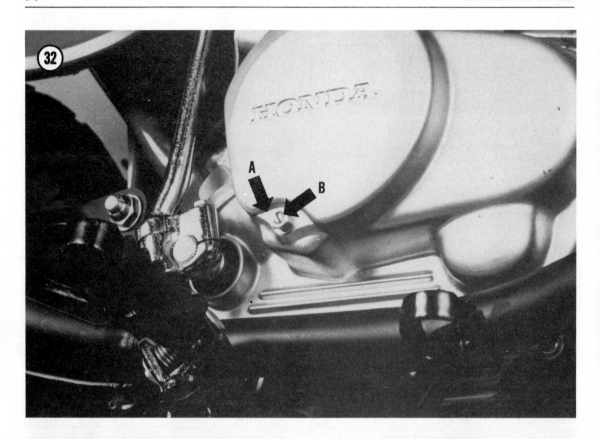

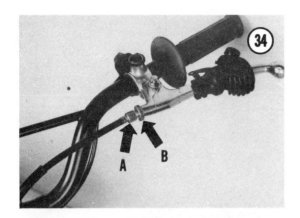

Clutch Cable Upper Adjuster

Loosen the locknut (A, **Figure 34**) on the clutch lever and turn the adjuster (B, **Figure 34**) in or out to obtain the correct amount of free play, tighten the locknut (A).

Road test the bike to make sure the clutch fully disengages when the lever is pulled in; if it does not, the bike will creep in gear when stopped. Also make sure the clutch fully engages; if it does not, the clutch will slip, particularly when accelerating in high gear.

Camshaft Chain Adjustment

After a period of time, which will vary with the amount of use the bike gets, the camshaft chain will become noisy and will need adjusting.

1. Start the engine and let it idle.

2. Loosen the set plate bolt (A, **Figure 35**) located on the cylinder head.

3. Rotate the adjuster screw (B, **Figure 35**) until the dot is straight up to 12 o'clock. At this point the chain is at its maximum looseness. Rotate the screw until the dot is straight down to 6 o'clock. The chain is now tightened to its maximum at this area of adjustment. The correct position is where the chain noise is minimal. Tighten the set plate bolt.

4. If the chain is still noisy with the dot at the 6 o'clock position, tighten the set plate bolt and turn the engine off.

5. Loosen the camshaft chain adjusting bolt locknut (C, **Figure 36**), and then the adjusting bolt (D, **Figure 36**) at the base of the cylinder.

6. Tighten the adjusting bolt and locknut.

7. Loosen the set plate bolt (A, **Figure 35**) and move the dot on the adjuster screw (B, **Figure 35**) to the 3 o'clock position.

8. Start the engine and turn the adjuster screw in either direction until chain noise is minimal.

9. Tighten the set plate bolt.

10. If the chain is still noisy after this procedure, it has become stretched and will have to be replaced. Refer to Chapter Five.

Drive Chain Adjustment

Every 30 operating days or three months, whichever comes first, the drive chain should be

adjusted. Proper chain tension is important. If the tension is too loose, the chain may skip while traveling at high speed. If tension is too tight, engine effort and chain wear increase.

The correct chain tension is measured by pressing on the bottom of the chain at midpoint. The slack should be ¾ in. (20mm). See **Figure 23**. If tension is incorrect, use the following adjustment procedure.

1. Block up the bike so that the rear wheel is off the ground.

2. Remove the cotter pin and loosen the axle nut (A, **Figure 37**).

3. Turn the adjusting nuts (B, **Figure 37**) in either direction. Turning the nut *clockwise* will increase tension and turning it *counterclockwise* will decrease tension.

4. The index mark on the adjuster must align with the same reference mark on the side scale on both right- and left-hand side (**Figure 38**).

5. Tighten the axle nut to 29-40 ft.-lb. (400-550 kg-cm) and install a new cotter pin. Be sure to bend over both ends of the pin completely.

> NOTE: *Make sure that the chain protector does not interfere with the drive chain.*

6. Check the rear brake operation as it may have to be adjusted. Refer to *Rear Brake Adjustment* in Chapter Seven.

Fuel Lines

Fuel lines can often carry dirt from the fuel tank to the carburetor. They also may become clogged and cause the carburetor to run lean. This could result in engine damage.

1. Turn the fuel shutoff valve to the OFF position.

2. Remove the fuel line from the shutoff valve (**Figure 39**) and carburetor.

3. Blow through the fuel line to clear any dirt or obstruction.

4. Replace the fuel line on the carburetor and fuel shutoff valve.

Wheels and Tires

Every 30 operating days or three months, whichever comes first, check the wheels for

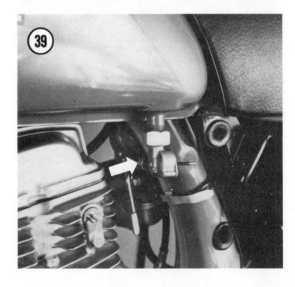

bent or damaged rims and loose or missing spokes. Check tires for any road damage or worn tread. Refer to Chapter Seven for complete wheel information.

Spokes

Spokes should be checked periodically for looseness or bending. Check spokes for proper tension. The "tuning fork" method for checking tension is simple and works well. Tap each spoke with a spoke wrench or screwdriver shank. A taut spoke will emit a clear, ringing tone; a loose spoke will sound flat. All spokes in a correctly tightened wheel will emit tones of similar pitch, but not necessarily the same tone.

Bent, stripped, or otherwise damaged spokes should be replaced as soon as they are detected. Refer to *Spokes* in Chapter Seven for spoke replacement.

Spokes tend to loosen as the motorcycle is used. If they are loose, retighten each spoke one turn, beginning with those on one side of the hub, then those on the other side.

Fasteners

Every 1,000 miles, check all nuts, screws, and bolts that secure parts to the frame, e.g., engine fairings, lights, fenders, etc., to make sure that they are tight.

STORAGE

Preparation

If you store the bike for an extended period of time, prepare it in the following way:

1. Warm up the engine and thoroughly drain the oil; refill with new oil.

2. Empty the fuel tank completely, turn the fuel shutoff valve to the OFF position.

3. Run the engine until the carburetor is empty.

4. Remove the spark plug and put a few drops of oil into the cylinder.

5. Turn the engine over with the kickstarter to spread the oil around in the cylinder.

6. Install the spark plug, only finger-tight and connect the spark plug wire.

7. Clean and lubricate all parts.

8. Dampen a cloth with light oil and wipe all metal parts or spray them with a light coat of WD-40. This will help protect against rust.

9. Cover the bike with a tarp or blanket.

After Storage

Before starting the engine after storage, remove the spark plug and squirt a small amount of fuel into the cylinder to help remove the oil coating. Install the spark plug but do not connect the spark plug wire. Crank the engine over a few times, then reconnect the spark plug wire and start the engine.

4

CHAPTER FIVE

ENGINE, CLUTCH, AND TRANSMISSION

The XR75 engine is an extremely compact air-cooled, single cylinder four-cycle with overhead valves operated by a chain-driven single overhead camshaft. Individual rocker arms operate each valve and are provided with adjusting screws for setting the valve to rocker arm clearance. The adjusting screws are accessible by removing the cam cover.

The ignition system consists of an external ignition coil mounted underneath the fuel tank with conventional contact breaker points and an automatic centrifugally-operated ignition advance. Power for the system is provided by a magneto driven off of the left end of the crankshaft.

The right end of the crankshaft drives a wet clutch through straight-cut primary-drive gears. The crankshaft also operates the engine's oil pump (and centrifugal oil filter on 1975-1976 models), all enclosed within the right-hand engine cover.

The engine is small for such an efficient unit, yet it is remarkable in its simplicity. This chapter provides complete service and overhaul procedures as well as detailed instructions in the various component repairs that may be necessary.

Tables 1 and 2 give specifications and tightening torques, respectively. Both are at the end of the chapter.

ENGINE PRINCIPLES

Figure 1 explains how the engine works. This will be helpful when troubleshooting or repairing your engine.

ENGINE COOLING

Cooling is provided by air passing over the cooling fins on the engine cylinder head and cylinder. Therefore it is important to keep these fins free from a buildup of dirt, oil, grease, and other foreign matter. Brush out the fins with a whisk broom or small paintbrush.

SERVICING ENGINE IN FRAME

Many components can be serviced while the engine is mounted in the frame:

a. Cylinder head

b. Cylinder and piston

c. Camshaft and rocker arms

d. Oil pump and filter

e. Gearshift mechanism

f. Clutch

g. Carburetor

h. Magneto

It is recommended that prior to engine removal and disassembly, the majority of parts

4-STROKE OPERATING PRINCIPLES   ①

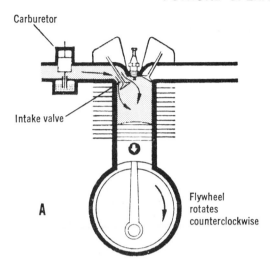

A

Flywheel rotates counterclockwise

As the piston travels downward, the exhaust valve is closed and the intake valve opens, allowing the new fuel/air mixture from the **carburetor** to be drawn into the cylinder. When the piston reaches the bottom of its travel (BDC), the **intake valve** closes and remains closed for the next revolution-and-a-half of the crankshaft.

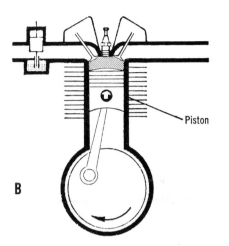

B

While the crankshaft continues to rotate, the **piston** moves upward, compressing the fuel/air mixture.

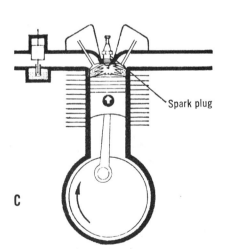

C

As the piston almost reaches the top of its travel, the **spark plug** fires, igniting the compressed fuel/air mixture. The piston continues to top dead center (TDC) and is pushed downward by the expanding gases.

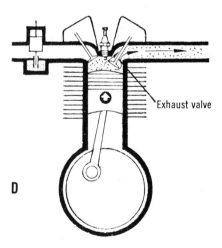

D

When the piston almost reaches BDC, the **exhaust valve** opens and remains open until the piston is near TDC. The upward travel of the piston causes the exhaust gases to be pushed out of the cylinder. After the piston has reached TDC, the exhaust valve closes and the cycle starts all over again.

be removed from the engine while it is still in the frame. In this way, the motorcycle frame itself can serve as an engine stand or holder and any operations requiring that the engine be secured in a benchstand or held by an assistant are thereby eliminated.

ENGINE

Removal/Installation

Prior to removal or disassembly of any major part of the engine, clean the entire area of all dirt, grease, and other foreign matter with Gunk Cycle Degreaser or equivalent. Follow the manufacturer's directions and avoid using too high of a water pressure when rinsing off the engine.

1. Drain the engine oil as described under *Changing Engine Oil* in Chapter Four.

2. Disconnect the spark plug wire and tie it up out of the way.

3. Remove the seat.

4. Turn the fuel shutoff valve to the OFF position and remove the fuel line to the carburetor.

5. Remove the fuel tank.

6. Remove carburetor as described under *Carburetor Removal/Installation* in Chapter Six.

7. Loosen the bolt securing the shift lever to the shaft and remove it.

8. Remove the exhaust system as described under *Exhaust System Removal/Installation* in Chapter Six.

9. Remove the left-hand engine cover.

10. Remove the 2 bolts securing the drive chain sprocket and remove the sprocket and chain.

11. Remove the electrical leads from the magneto to the wiring harness.

12. Remove the magneto as described under *Magneto Removal/Installation* in this chapter.

13. Remove the clutch cable from the right-hand engine cover.

14. Remove the clutch as described under *Clutch Removal/Installation* in this chapter.

15. Remove the cylinder head and cylinder as described under *Cylinder Removal/Installation* in this chapter.

16. Take a final look all over the engine to make sure everything has been disconnected.

NOTE: *Place wooden blocks under the crankcase to support the engine after the mounting bolt has been removed.*

17. Remove the remaining bolt on the lower rear and remove the engine from the frame; take it to a workbench for further disassembly.

18. Install by reversing the removal steps.

19. Tighten the engine mounting bolts to specifications in **Table 2**.

20. Fill the crankcase with the recommended type and quantity of engine oil; refer to Chapter Four.

CYLINDER HEAD

Removal

1. Remove the seat and fuel tank.

2. Remove the 2 nuts (A, **Figure 2**) securing the exhaust pipe to the cylinder head. Remove the swing arm pivot bolt nut (B, **Figure 2**) securing the muffler and remove it and the exhaust pipe.

3. Remove the 3 acorn nuts on 1975-1976 models, or 2 bolts on 1977 and later models (**Figure 3**), securing the cam cover and remove it.

4. Remove the 6 screws (**Figure 4**) securing the left-hand engine cover and remove it.

5. Rotate the engine by turning the magneto rotor until the "O" timing mark on the cam-

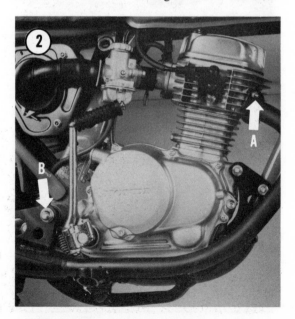

shaft sprocket (**Figure 5**) aligns with the mark on the camshaft and rocker arm housing on 1975-1976 models. On 1977 and later, the "O" mark should be at the 12 o'clock position.

6. Remove the 2 bolts securing the camshaft sprocket to the camshaft; remove the sprocket.

> NOTE: *To prevent the camshaft from turning, hold the magneto rotor with a strap wrench (Figure 6).*

7. Secure the camshaft chain to the frame with a piece of wire. Do not let it drop into the crankcase.

> NOTE: *There are a number of design differences in the rocker arm and camshaft holders. On 1975-1976 models, the holder completely captures the camshaft (Figure 7) and is removed as a unit. On 1977 and later models, the holder only secures the camshaft onto the cylinder head. The disassembly of the rocker arms is the same for both models.*

8. On 1975-1976 models, remove the 4 nuts securing the camshaft holder and lift it out.

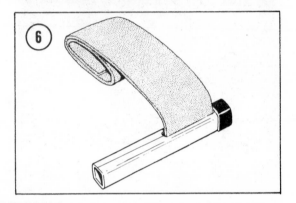

9. On 1977 and later models, remove the 4 nuts securing the camshaft holder and lift it out (**Figure 8**). Remove the camshaft.

10. Remove the locking bolt and tab and remove the cam chain tension adjusting bolt (**Figure 9**).

11. Remove the spark plug wire and spark plug.

12. Remove the carburetor attaching clip and pull the carburetor out of the rubber inlet pipe.

13. Remove the drive chain master link. Pry off the outer clip with a thin bladed screwdriver. Remove the outside plate and push in the inside plate, complete with the pins, out through the back of the chain.

14. Loosen all engine mounting bolts (**Figure 10**). Remove the front 4 and the upper rear. *Do not* remove the lower rear as it is used for a pivot.

> NOTE: *It is necessary to pivot the engine down in order to remove the cylinder head with the engine in the frame (**Figure 11**).*

5

15. On 1977 and later models, remove the additional bolt on the left-hand side of the head (**Figure 12**).

16. Remove the camshaft adjusting eccentric from the cylinder head (**Figure 13**).

17. Loosen the head by tapping around the perimeter with a plastic or rubber mallet.

CAUTION

*Remember the cooling fins are fragile and may be damaged if struck too hard. **Do not** use a metal hammer.*

NOTE: *Sometimes it is possible to loosen the head with the engine compression. Install the spark plug and rotate the engine with the kickstarter. As the piston reaches* TDC *on the compression stroke, the head will pop loose.*

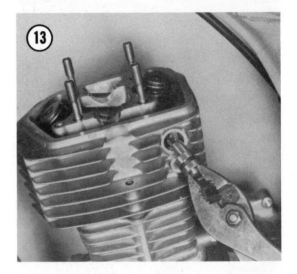

18. Slide the cylinder head straight up and off the cylinder studs (**Figure 14**).

19. Remove the cylinder head gasket, O-ring, and the dowel pins.

20. Place a clean shop rag into the cam chain slot to prevent the entry of foreign matter.

Inspection

1. Remove all traces of gasket from head and cylinder mating surface.

2. Without removing the valves, remove all carbon deposits from the combustion chambers with a wire brush. A blunt screwdriver or chisel may be used if care is taken not to damage the head of valves.

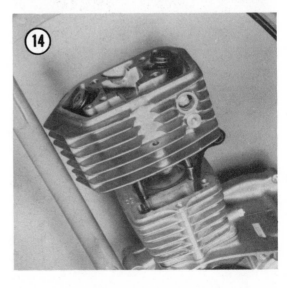

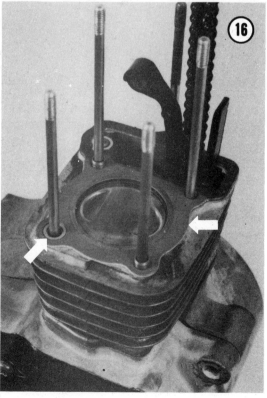

3. After all carbon is removed from combustion chamber, valve intake and exhaust ports, clean the entire head in solvent.

4. Clean away all carbon on the piston crown. *Do not remove carbon ridge at the top of the cylinder bore.*

5. Check for cracks in the combustion chamber and exhaust ports. Cracked heads must be replaced.

6. Check the condition of the valves and the valve seats as described under *Valves and Valve Seats* in this chapter.

Installation

1. Install the two locating dowels in the top of the cylinder (**Figure 15**).

2. Install the head gasket and O-ring (**Figure 16**).

3. Carefully lower the cylinder head over the cylinder studs and onto the locating dowels. Pull the cam chain up through the opening in the cylinder head with the wire used to hold it in place during removal.

> CAUTION
> *Be sure that the rubber O-ring in the head gasket does not slip out of place during assembly.*

4. On 1975-1976 models, install the camshaft holder.

5. On 1977 and later models, coat the bearing surfaces of the camshaft with engine oil and install the camshaft (**Figure 8**). Install the camshaft holder.

6. Install 4 flat washers and nuts. Tighten nuts in crisscross pattern to torque of 5.8-8.7 ft.-lb. (8-12 N•m).

> CAUTION
> *On 1975-1976 models, the right rear nut securing the camshaft holder is an acorn type with a "soft" washer since the right rear cylinder stud is used as a passageway for the lubrication system. If the "soft" washer and acorn nut are not replaced in the same location, damage to the valve gear could result due to a loss of oil pressure.*

7. Lift the cam chain and install the cam sprocket.

5

8. Rotate the camshaft so that both cam lobes are farthest away from contact with the rocker arms. They should be in the 4 o'clock and 8 o'clock positions.

9. Rotate the magneto rotor until the "T" mark on the rotor aligns with the pointer on the engine side cover. See **Figure 17** for 1975-1976 models and **Figure 18** for 1977 and later models.

10. Without turning the crankshaft from the "T" position on the magneto rotor, fit the camshaft sprocket within the cam chain with the "O" mark at the top. See **Figure 19**. This should locate the holes in the sprocket in approximately the same position as the holes in the end of the camshaft and directly in line with the gasket surface of the cylinder head.

11. Fit the camshaft sprocket on the end of the camshaft and install the two bolts. The dowel bolt fits in the right hole. Tighten the bolts to between 7.3 and 11.6 ft.-lbs. (10-16 N•m). Once the bolts are right, double check the "T" mark on the flywheel and the "O" mark on the sprocket to see that they have not moved relative to their pointers.

> NOTE: *Correct valve timing depends on the proper relationship of all of parts in Steps 8-11.*

> CAUTION
> *Very expensive damage could result from improper installation.*

12. Complete the installation by reversing removal Steps 10-16 and Steps 1-4.

13. When installing the master link on the drive chain, use a new master link clip and install it with the opening facing the opposite direction of chain travel **(Figure 20)**. Incorrect installation will result in the loss of the clip and may result in chain breakage.

14. Tighten all engine mounting bolts to 14.5-22 ft.-lb. (10-16 N•m).

15. Adjust the valve clearance as described under *Valve Clearance Adjustment* in Chapter Four.

16. Adjust the camshaft chain as described under *Camshaft Chain Adjustment* in Chapter Four.

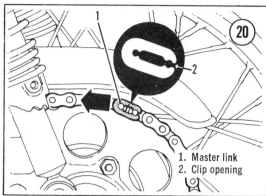

1. Master link
2. Clip opening

17. Start the engine and check for leaks.

VALVES AND VALVE SEATS

Removal

1. Remove cylinder heads as described under *Cylinder Head Removal* in this chapter.

2. Compress springs with a valve spring compression tool (**Figure 21**), remove the valve keepers (**Figure 22**) and release compression.

3. Remove the valve spring caps, springs, and valves (**Figure 23**).

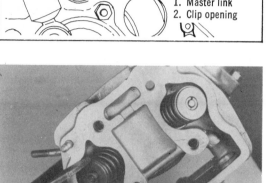

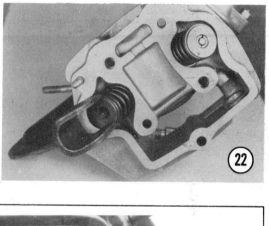

1. Keepers
2. Cap
3. Valve springs
4. Valve

1   2   3   4

CAUTION
Remove any burrs from the valve stem grooves before removing the valve. Otherwise the valve guides will be damaged.

Inspection

1. Clean valves with a wire brush and solvent.

2. Inspect the contact surface of each valve for burning (**Figure 24**). Minor roughness and pitting can be removed by lapping the valve as described under *Valve Lapping* in this chapter. Excessive unevenness to the contact surface is an indication that the valve is not serviceable. The contact surface of the valve may be ground on a valve grinding machine, but it is best to replace any burned or damaged valve with a new one.

Inspect the valve stems for wear and roughness and measure the vertical runout of the valve face as shown in **Figure 25**. The runout should not exceed 0.001 in. (0.025mm).

3. Measure the valve stems for wear. Compare with specifications in **Table 1** at the end of the chapter.

4. Remove all carbon and varnish from the valve guides with a stiff spiral wire brush.

5. Insert each valve in its guide. Hold the valve just slightly off its seats and rock it sideways. If it rocks more than slightly, the guide is probably worn and should be replaced. As a final check, take the head to a dealer and have the valve guides measured.

6. Measure the valve spring heights with a vernier caliper (**Figure 26**). All should be of length specified in **Table 1** with no bends or other distortion. Replace defective springs.

7. Check the valve spring retainer and valve keepers. If they are in good condition, they may be reused.

8. Inspect valve seats. If worn or burned, they must be reconditioned. This should be performed by your dealer or local machine shop, although the procedure is described later in this section. Seats and valves in near-perfect condition can be reconditioned by lapping with fine carborundum paste. Lapping, however, is always inferior to precision grinding.

Installation

1. Coat the valve stems with molybdenum disulphide paste and insert them into cylinder head.

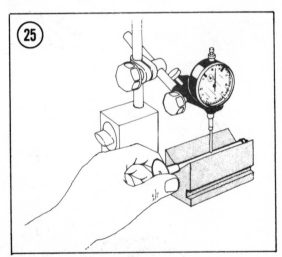

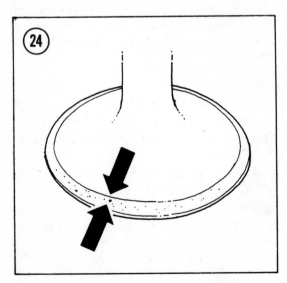

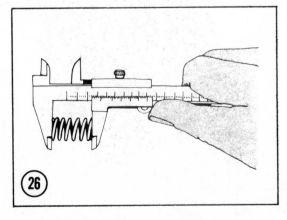

2. Install bottom spring retainers and new seals.

3. Install valve springs and upper valve spring retainers.

4. Push down on upper valve spring retainers with the valve spring compressor and install valve keepers.

Valve Guide Replacement

When guides are worn so that there is excessive stem-to-guide clearance or valve tipping, they must be replaced. Replace all, even if only one is worn. This job should only be done by a Honda dealer as special tools are required.

Valve Seat Reconditioning

This job is best left to your dealer or local machine shop. They have the special equipment and knowledge for this exacting job. You can still save considerable money by removing the cylinder head and taking just the head to the shop.

Valve Lapping

Valve lapping is a simple operation which can restore the valve seal without machining if the amount of wear or distortion is not too great.

1. Coat the valve seating area in the head with a lapping compound such as carborundum or Clover Brand.

2. Insert the valve into the head.

3. Wet the suction cup of the lapping stick (**Figure 27**) and stick it onto the head of the valve. Lap the valve to the seat by rotating the lapping stick in both directions. Every 5 to 10 seconds, rotate the valve 180° in the seat; continue lapping until the contact surfaces of the valve and the valve seat are a uniform grey. Stop as soon as they are to avoid removing too much material.

4. Thoroughly clean the valves and cylinder head in solvent to remove all grinding compound. Any compound left on the valves or the cylinder head will end up in the engine and will cause damage.

CAMSHAFT AND ROCKER ASSEMBLIES

The camshaft is driven by a chain off of the timing sprocket on the transmission countershaft.

It is important that all parts be assembled in their original positions. Therefore, before disassembling, mark the parts in some way to remind you later.

Disassembly (1975-1976 Models)

1. Perform Steps 1-8 of *Cylinder Head Removal*, in this chapter, to remove the camshaft holder.

2. Remove the bolt securing the camshaft in the camshaft holder (**Figure 28**).

3. Remove the camshaft.

4. Thread an 8mm bolt into the end of the rocker arm shaft (**Figure 29**).

5. Pull the shaft free with the bolt.

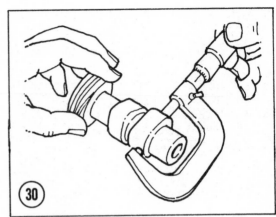

6. Repeat the procedure for the other rocker arm shaft.

Disassembly (1977 and Later Models)

1. Perform Steps 1-9 of *Cylinder Head Removal*, in this chapter, to remove the camshaft holder.

2. Hold the camshaft holder and tap it with a soft hammer. This will cause the rocker arm shafts to move free of the holder.

3. Remove the shafts and the rocker arms.

> NOTE: *The rocker arm shafts are of different lengths. The intake shaft is the longer and has a relief in one end to provide clearance for one of the cylinder head studs. Be sure that the camshaft holder is reassembled with the shafts in their proper position and that the rocker arms are not interchanged.*

4. Clean all parts in cleaning solvent and thoroughly dry.

Rocker Inspection

1. Carefully inspect the rocker arm bore and bearing faces for signs of wear or scoring. Measure the inside diameter of the rocker arm bore with a micrometer and compare them to the dimension of the rocker arm shaft. See Step 3.

2. Inspect the rocker shafts for signs of wear or scoring.

3. Measure the outside diameter with a micrometer and check against the dimension in Step 1. If the difference between the two dimen-

sions is 0.0039 in. (0.1mm) or greater, either one or both parts should be replaced.

Camshaft Inspection

1. Check the bearing journals for wear and scoring.

2. Check cam lobes for wear. The lobes should not be scored and the edges should be square. Slight damage may be removed with a silicon carbide oilstone. Use No. 100-120 grit initially, then polish with a No. 280-320 grit.

3. Measure the height of each cam lobe with a micrometer as shown in **Figure 30**. Replace the shaft if worn beyond the serviceable limit (measurements less than those given in **Table 1**).

Assembly

1. Coat the rocker arm shafts, rocker arm bores, and the camshaft holder bores with assembly lubricant or engine oil.

2. Hold the intake rocker arm in its approximate position in the camshaft holder and slide the intake rocker arm shaft (the long one on later models) through the camshaft holder and the rocker arm bore. Make sure that the semicircle relief matches with the cylinder head stud hole.

3. Install the exhaust rocker arm and rocker arm shaft.

4. Install the camshaft in the camshaft holder and tighten the securing bolt (1975-1976 models only).

5. Complete the installation by performing Steps 4-17, 1975-1976 models, and Steps 5-17 on 1977 and later models.

CYLINDER

Removal

1. Remove the cylinder head as described under *Cylinder Head Removal* in this chapter.

2. Remove the cam chain guide (**Figure 31**).

3. Slide the cylinder and cam chain tensioner straight up and off the cylinder studs (**Figure 32**).

> NOTE: *If the cylinder is stuck, tap it gently on the cooling fins with a plastic or rubber mallet.*

CAUTION
The cooling fins are fragile and may be damaged if struck too hard. **Do not** *use a metal hammer.*

4. Be sure to keep the cam chain wired up to the frame. Do not let it fall into the crankcase.

5. Place a clean shop cloth into the crankcase opening to prevent the entry of small parts and foreign matter.

6. Remove the alignment dowel.

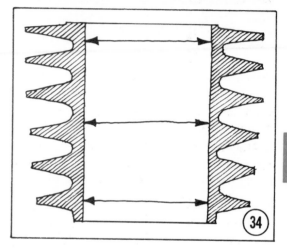

Inspection

Measure the cylinder bore, with a cylinder gauge (**Figure 33**) or inside micrometer, at the points shown in **Figure 34**.

Measure in two axes — in line with the wrist pin and at 90° to the pin. If the taper or out-of-round is 0.004 in. (0.10mm) or greater, the cylinder must be rebored to the next oversize and new piston installed.

> NOTE: *The new piston should be obtained first before the cylinder is bored so that pistons can be measured; slight manufacturing tolerances must be taken into account to determine the actual size and the working clearance. The piston-to-cylinder clearance should be 0.0035-0.0040 in. (0.089-0.10mm).*

Installation

1. Install a new base gasket and install the dowel pins (**Figure 35**).

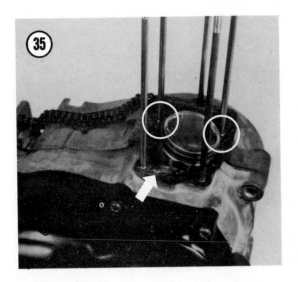

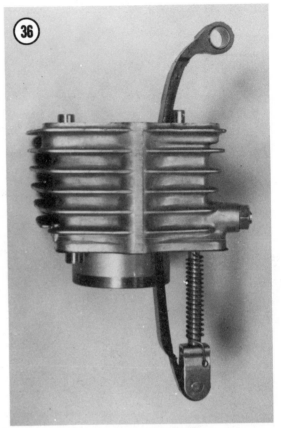

2. Install the cam chain tensioner in the cylinder cam chain cavity (**Figure 36**).

3. Install a piston holding fixture under the piston (**Figure 37**) to hold the piston in position while installing the cylinder.

> NOTE: *These fixtures may be purchased or may be homemade units of wood. See* Figure 38.

4. Pull the cam chain up through the cylinder and secure it to the frame.

5. Carefully slide the cylinder down over the piston. Compress each piston ring, with your fingers, as the cylinder starts to slide over it.

6. Remove the piston holding fixtures and push the cylinder down all the way (**Figure 39**).

7. Install the cam chain guide (**Figure 40**).

8. Install the cylinder head as described under *Cylinder Head Installation* in this chapter.

PISTON AND CONNECTING ROD

The piston may be removed with the engine in the frame by removing the cylinder head and the cylinder. To remove the rod the crankcase has to be split in order to gain access to the crankshaft.

Piston Removal

1. Remove the cylinder head and cylinder as described under *Cylinder Removal/Installation* in this chapter.

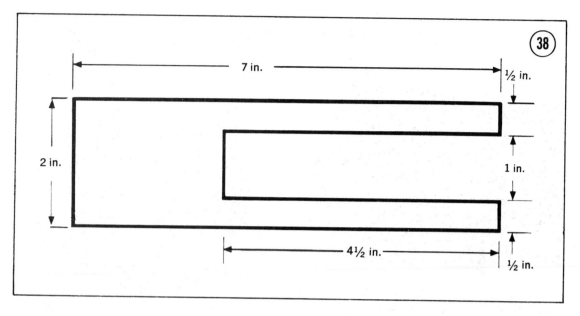

7 in. ½ in. 2 in. 1 in. 4½ in. ½ in.

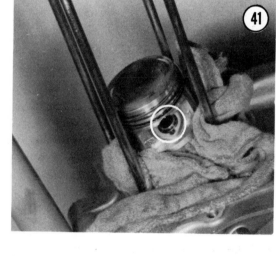

2. Remove one of the wrist pin circlips with needle nose pliers (**Figure 41**). Wrap a clean shop cloth under the piston so that the clip will not drop into the crankcase.

3. Before removing the piston, hold the rod tightly and rock the piston as shown in **Figure 42**. Any rocking motion (do not confuse with the normal sliding motion) indicates wear on the wrist pin, rod bushing, pin bore or more likely, a combination of all three. If the pin is to be reused, mark it so it will be installed in the same position.

4. Remove the top ring first by spreading the ends with your thumbs just enough to slide it up

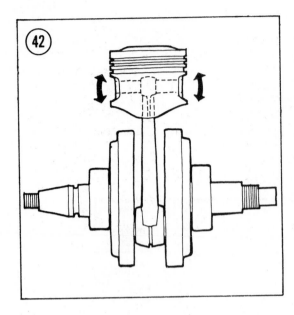

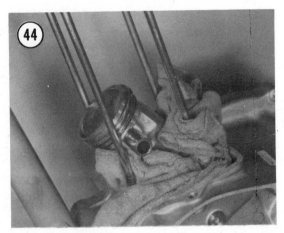

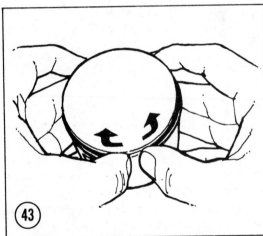

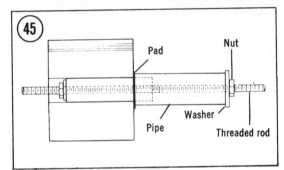

over the piston (**Figure 43**). Repeat for the remaining rings.

5. Push the wrist pin out of the piston and connecting rod and remove the piston assembly (**Figure 44**).

> CAUTION
>
> *Do not use excessive force removing the wrist pin since this could cause damage to the connecting rod.*

6. If the pin is tight, heat the piston with a propane torch, to about 140°F (60°C), i.e., until it is too warm to touch, but not excessively hot. The pin will probably fall out. If the pin is still difficult to push out, use a homemade tool as shown in **Figure 45**.

Piston Inspection

1. Carefully clean the carbon from the piston crown with a chemical remover or with a soft scraper (**Figure 46**). *Do not* remove or damage the carbon ridge around the circumference of the piston above the top ring. If the piston, rings, and cylinder are found to be dimensionally correct and can be reused, removal of the carbon ring from the top of piston of the carbon ridge from the top of cylinder will promote excessive oil consumption.

(47)

WARNING
*The rail portions of the oil scraper can
be very sharp. Be careful when handling
them to avoid cut fingers.*

CAUTION
Do not wire brush the piston skirt.

2. Examine each ring groove for burrs, dented
edges, and wide wear. Pay particular attention
to the top compression ring groove, as it usually
wears more than the others.

3. Measure piston-to-cylinder clearance as
described under *Piston Clearance* in this
chapter.

4. If damage or wear indicates piston replacement, select a new piston as described under
Piston Clearance in this chapter.

5. Measure any parts marked in Step 4 of the
Piston Removal procedure with a micrometer
and dial bore gauge to determine which part or
parts are worn. Check against measurements
given in **Table 2**. Any machinist can do this for
you if you do not have micrometers. Replace
piston/pin set as a unit if either or both are
worn.

Piston Clearance

1. Make sure the piston and cylinder walls are
clean and dry.

2. Measure the inside diameter of the cylinder
bore at a point ½ in. (13mm) from the upper
edge with a bore gauge (**Figure 33**).

3. Measure the outside diameter of the piston
at a point ⅝ in. (15mm) from the lower edge of
the piston 90° to the piston pin axis (**Figure 47**).
Check against measurement given in **Table 2**.

Connecting Rod Removal

In order to remove the rods, the crankcase
has to be split. Refer to *Crankcase Disassembly*
in this chapter.

Connecting Rod Inspection

1. Check the rod for obvious damage such as
cracks and burns.

2. Check the piston pin bushing for wear or
scoring.

3. Take the rod to a machine shop and have
them check alignment for twisting and bending.

Assembly

1. Coat the connecting rod bushing, piston pin, and piston hole with assembly lubricant.

2. Place the piston over the connecting rod with the IN (intake) marking (**Figure 48**) toward the rear of the engine. If the same wrist pin is to be used, install it in the same position as it was before. Refer to the index mark made in Step 3 of *Piston Removal*.

3. Insert the piston pin and tap it with a plastic mallet until it starts into the connecting rod bushing. If it does not slide in easily, heat the piston until it is too warm to touch but not excessively hot (140°F or 60°C). Continue to drive the piston in while holding the piston so that the rod does not have to take any shock. Otherwise, it may be bent. Drive the pin in until it is centered in the rod. If pin is still difficult to install, use the homemade tool (**Figure 45**) but eliminate the piece of pipe.

4. Install rings as described in Steps 3-8 under *Piston Ring Replacement*.

PISTON RINGS

Replacement

1. Remove old rings with a ring expander tool or by spreading the ring ends with your thumbs and lifting the rings up evenly (**Figure 43**).

2. Carefully remove all carbon from the ring grooves. Inspect grooves carefully for burrs, nicks, or broken and cracked lands. Recondition or replace piston if necessary.

3. Check end gap of each ring. To check ring, insert the ring into the bottom of the cylinder bore and square it with the wall by tapping with the piston. The ring should be in about ⅝ in. (15mm). Insert a feeler gauge as shown in **Figure 49**. Compare gap with **Table 2**. If the gap is smaller than specified, hold a small file in a vise, grip the ends of the ring with your fingers, and enlarge the gap. See **Figure 50**.

4. Roll each ring around its piston groove as shown in **Figure 51** to check for binding. Minor binding may be cleaned up with a fine cut file.

NOTE: *Install all rings with their markings facing up.*

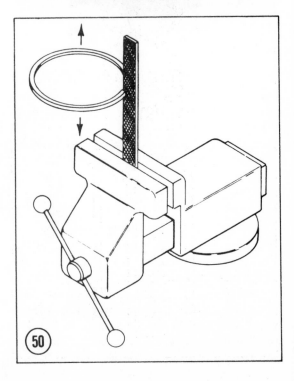

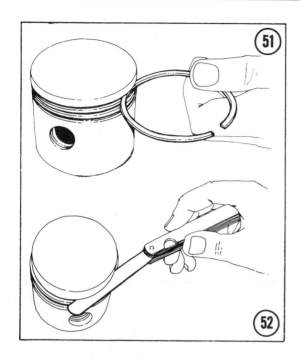

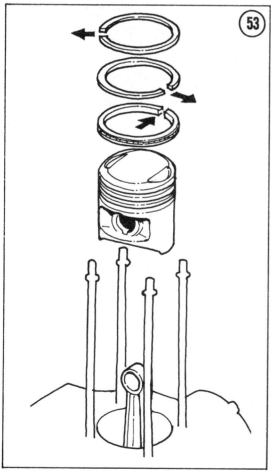

5. Install oil ring in oil ring groove with a ring expander tool or spread the ends with your thumbs.

6. Install 2 compression rings carefully with a ring expander tool or spread the ends with your thumbs.

7. Check side clearance of each ring as shown in **Figure 52**. Compare with specifications in **Table 2**.

8. Distribute ring gaps around piston as shown in **Figure 53**. The important thing is that the ring gaps are not aligned with each other when installed.

PRIMARY DRIVE

Disassembly/Assembly

1. Remove the footrest assembly and the kickstarter lever (**Figure 54**). Remove the clutch cable from the clutch lever (**Figure 55**).

2. Place a drip pan under the engine and remove the drain plug (**Figure 56**). Drain all the oil.

3. Loosen, then remove the 9 screws (**Figure 57**) securing the right-hand engine cover and remove it.

> NOTE: *There will still be some oil inside the engine cover; place drip pan under the lower seam prior to removing it.*

4. Tap the engine cover gently with a plastic or rubber mallet and remove it. Remove the locating dowels (**Figure 58**).

5. Remove the oil through the pipe and spring in the end of the crankshaft (**Figure 59**).

6. On 1975-1976 models, an oil filter rotor is used. Remove the 3 screws (**Figure 60**) securing the filter cover and remove it.

7. Insert a "soft" wedge, such as aluminum or wood, between the 2 primary drive gears to keep them from turning (**Figure 61**).

8. On 1975-1976 models, use a special tool (Honda part No. 07086-00102, see **Figure 62**)

S = Short
M = Medium
L = Long

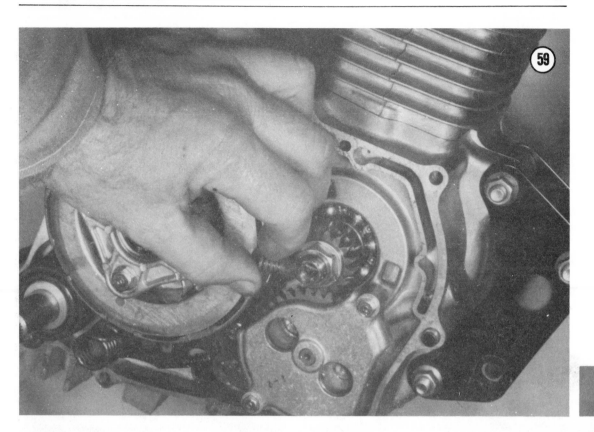

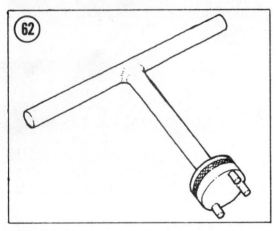

and remove the locknut securing the oil filter rotor (**Figure 61**) and remove it.

9. On 1976 and later models, remove the nut and lockwasher (**Figure 63**).

> NOTE: *The oil filter rotor and rotor cover will have oil sludge residue in them. Clean with cleaning solvent and thoroughly dry.*

10. Assemble by reversing the disassembly steps.

11. Tighten the primary drive gear nut to 25-33 ft.-lb. (34-45 N•m).

12. Fill the crankcase with the recommended type and quantity of oil. Refer to *Changing Engine Oil* in Chapter Four.

CLUTCH

Disassembly

1. Complete Steps 1-4 of *Primary Drive Disassembly/Assembly* in this chapter.

2. Remove the 4 bolts, slowly in a crisscross pattern, securing the clutch lifter plate.

3. Remove the guide pin (**Figure 64**) and lifter plate (**Figure 65**).

4. Remove the 4 clutch springs (**Figure 66**).

5. Remove the snap ring securing the clutch center (**Figure 67**).

6. Remove the clutch center and clutch plates (**Figure 68**).

7. Remove the splined washer (**Figure 69**).

8. Remove the outer clutch cover/primary gear assembly (**Figure 70**).

> NOTE: *Some models may have a spacer behind the clutch cover/primary gear assembly; if so remove it.*

Inspection

1. Clean all clutch parts in petroleum-based solvent, such as kerosene, and thoroughly dry with compressed air.

2. Measure the free length of each clutch spring (**Figure 71**). New springs measure 1.0748 in. (27.3mm). Replace the springs that are 0.9961 in. (25.3mm) or less.

3. Measure the thickness of each friction disc at several places around the disc as shown in **Figure 72**. Compare them to the measurements in **Table 2**. Replace any that are worn to the wear limit.

4. Check all parts for signs of wear or other damage. Replace any parts as necessary. Make sure that the bearing runs free without any signs of roughness in its rotation.

Installation

Install by reversing the removal steps and noting the following steps.

1. After installing the outer clutch cover/ primary gear assembly, spline washer, and

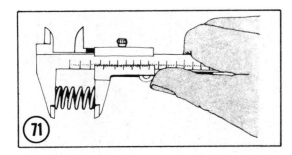

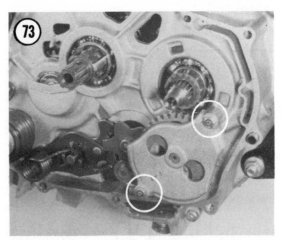

clutch pressure plate, install the clutch plates. Start with a friction disc and alternate the clutch plates and friction discs until all five are installed.

> NOTE: *Make sure that the splines of the clutch plates and the splines of the clutch center align.*

2. Install the 4 bolts in a crisscross pattern a little at a time until all are tight.

3. Complete installation by reversing *Primary Drive Disassembly/Assembly* Steps 1-4 as described in this chapter.

OIL PUMP

This procedure is shown on a 1977 model. The removal/installation steps are the same for all models except as noted in Steps 1 and 2. The oil pump gear cover is different in appearance only.

This procedure is shown with the clutch assembly removed for clarity; it is not necessary

to remove it for oil pump removal and installation.

Removal/Installation

1. Complete Steps 1-8 of *Primary Drive Removal/Installation* in this chapter.

2. Remove the 2 bolts securing the oil pump gear cover (**Figure 73**) and remove it.

3. Remove the tachometer pinion gear (1975-1976 models only) and the oil pump drive gear (**Figure 74**).

4. Remove the 2 bolts securing the oil pump body (**Figure 75**) and remove it.

5. Carefully remove the 2 rubber O-rings (**Figure 76**).

6. Remove the oil filter screen (**Figure 77**).

7. Install by reversing the removal steps. Be sure to use new O-rings and make sure they are completely seated when installed.

Inspection

1. Check the housing for cracks or fractures.

2. Measure the clearance between the outer rotor and the pump body with a flat feeler gauge.

3. Measure the clearance between the inner and outer rotor with a flat feeler gauge.

4. If clearances found in Steps 2 and 3, above, are 0.0079 in. (0.2mm) or greater, the worn parts must be replaced.

SHIFTER MECHANISM

Removal/Installation

1. Remove the clutch as described under *Clutch Removal/Installation* in this chapter.

2. Remove the oil pump as described under *Oil Pump Removal/Installation* in this chapter.

3. Loosen, approximately 3 to 4 turns, the bolt securing the detent arm (**Figure 78**).

4. Flip the pawl out of the cam plate and disengage the spring from under the pawl (**Figure 79**).

5. Remove the bolt securing the detent arm and remove it.

6. Remove the bolt securing the cam plate (**Figure 80**) and remove it.

7. Carefully remove the gear shift spindle (**Figure 81**) and return spring.

8. Install by reversing the removal steps.

MAGNETO

Removal/Installation

1. Remove the 5 screws securing the left-hand engine cover (**Figure 82**) and remove it.

2. Remove the nut securing the rotor to the crankshaft.

> NOTE: *To prevent the rotor from turning, hold it with a strap wrench (Figure 83) or a special tool (Figure 84).*

3. Remove the flywheel with a flywheel puller (Honda part No. 07016-00102). See **Figure 85**. The flywheel puller has left-hand threads so it must be installed counterclockwise. Screw the outer body in until it stops. Hold the outer

5

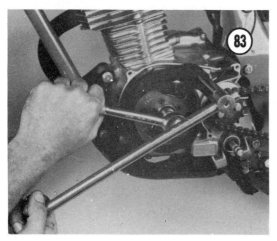

body stationary with a wrench and turn the inner body **(Figure 86)** until the rotor disengages from the crankshaft. Remove the rotor **(Figure 87)**.

4. Remove 2 screws **(Figure 88)** which secure the contact breaker point plate onto the stator.

5. Disconnect the electrical wire from the magneto to the wiring harness, pull the rubber grommet out of the crankcase slot **(Figure 89)** and remove the assembly.

6. Remove the Woodruff key in the crankshaft.

7. Install by reversing the removal steps. Be sure to install the Woodruff key. When installing the rotor be careful to align the slot in the rotor with the Woodruff key.

8. Tighten the rotor nut to 22-28 ft.-lb. (30-38 N•m).

9. Check and adjust the timing as described under *Magneto Ignition Timing and Contact Breaker Point Adjustment* in Chapter Four.

CRANKCASE

Service to the lower end and transmission requires that the crankcase assembly be removed from the motorcycle frame.

While the engine is still in the frame, it is easier to remove the cylinder head, cylinder, piston, magneto, and clutch assembly. In addition, the decrease of engine weight makes it easier to remove the crankcase from the frame.

Disassembly

1. After all of the above items have been removed, *loosen* the 2 remaining crankcase screws (**Figure 90**).

2. Remove the kickstarter spring (A, **Figure 91**) and spacer (B, **Figure 91**).

3. Take a final look all over the engine to make sure everything has been removed.

> NOTE: *Place wooden blocks under the crankcase to support the engine after the mounting bolt has been removed.*

4. Remove the remaining bolt on the lower rear and remove the engine from the frame; take it to workbench for further disassembly.

5. Remove the 2 remaining crankcase screws (**Figure 90**). Hold the crankcase assembly by the right-hand cylinder studs and tap on the end of the crankshaft and transmission mainshaft with a plastic or rubber mallet (**Figure 92**).

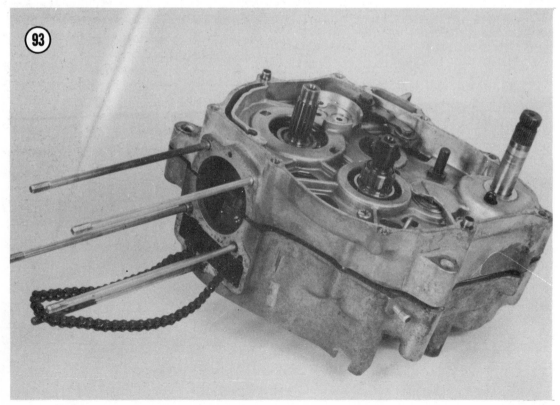

5

CAUTION

*Any excess force applied during disassembly of the crankcase halves may cause permanent damage to them. Tap both shaft ends and around the perimeter of the cases, moving them apart a little at a time (**Figure 93**). **Do not** pry them apart with a screwdriver or any metal object.*

6. Remove the crankshaft assembly from the left-hand crankcase half (**Figure 94**).

7. Remove the cam chain.

8. Remove the kickstarter gear and shaft (**Figure 95**).

NOTE: *Slowly rotate the shaft counter-clockwise while removing.*

9. Remove the shift fork shaft (**Figure 96**).
10. Remove the shift forks (A, **Figure 97**).

> NOTE: *On 1977 and later models, engine No. XR75E-140001 and later, a 5-speed transmission is used. The differences include a different gear set, three shifter forks and different shift drum. Disassembly and assembly procedures are the same.*

11. Remove the shift drum (B, **Figure 97**).

12. Remove the mainshaft (A, **Figure 98**) and countershaft (B, **Figure 98**) as an assembly.

13. Remove all traces of old side cover and cylinder base gaskets. Thoroughly clean the inside and outside of both crankcase halves with cleaning solvent. Dry with compressed air; make sure there is no solvent residue left inside the cases as it will contaminate new engine oil.

Assembly

Prior to assembly, be sure that all components are thoroughly cleaned and subassemblies such as the transmission gear sets are properly assembled.

1. Apply engine oil to the transmission bearings in both crankcase halves (**Figures 99 and 100**).

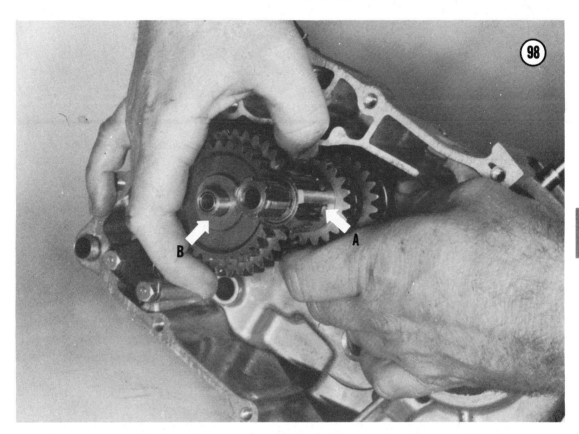

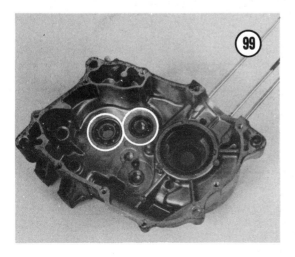

2. Install the mainshaft and countershaft gear sets into the left-hand crankcase half as an assembly (**Figure 101**).

3. Install the shift drum. Locate the drum with the neutral switch rotor toward the neutral switch (**Figure 102**).

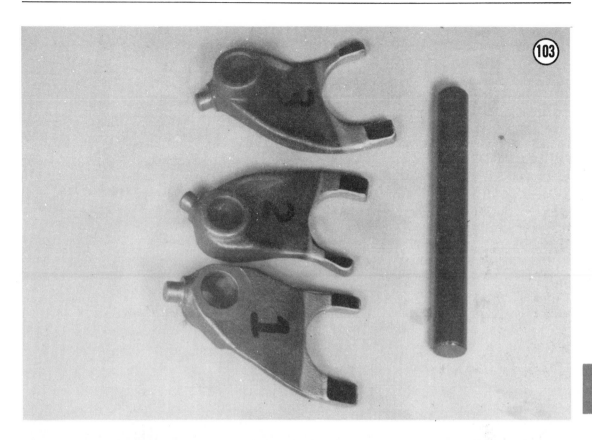

4. Install the left shift fork (No. 1, **Figure 103**) into the groove in the countershaft top gear. Lift the fork and gear until the guide pin drops into the slot in the shift drum. Slightly turn the shift fork to ease the installation.

> NOTE: *On 1975-1976 models with 4-speed transmissions and only 2 shift forks, the first shift fork is installed in the mainshaft 3rd gear.*

5. Install center shift fork (No. 2, **Figure 103**) into groove in the countershaft 3rd gear.

> NOTE: *On 1975-1976 models, the second shift fork fits into the groove in the countershaft 2nd gear.*

6. Install the right shift fork (No. 3, **Figure 103**) into the groove in the countershaft 4th gear.

7. Install the shift fork shaft through each shift fork and into the crankcase. Be sure that the forks are still in the proper gear and that the guide pin portion of the fork is in the slot in the shift drum (**Figure 104**).

8. Once assembled, rotate each shaft to be sure they rotate smoothly without any binding.

9. On 1975-1976 models, install the kickstarter spindle and hook the end of the spring over the lug on the crankcase (**Figure 105**). Temporarily install the kickstarter lever onto the shaft and rotate the lever with hand. Fit the kickstarter retainer down into the recess in the crankcase with the other hand.

10. On 1977 and later models, install the kickstarter shaft assembly into the crankcase and rotate clockwise so that the starter ratchet stopper is positioned under the guide plate (**Figure 95**).

11. Place the cam chain in the left crankcase half.

12. Install the crankshaft assembly (**Figure 106**) into the crankcase and loop the chain over the timing sprocket on the crankshaft (**Figure 107**).

CAUTION
When installing the crankshaft, make sure that the connecting rod is in the

open portion of the crankcase. If it is not, the crankshaft bearing will not bottom in the crankcase.

13. Install the 2 dowel pins and new gasket on the left-hand crankcase half (**Figue 108**).

14. Carefully lower the right-hand crankcase half over the shafts and down against the left-hand crankcase half.

NOTE: *On 1975-1976 models, be sure that the starter pinion friction spring (Figure 109) is in the locating recess in the right-hand crankcase half.*

Tap around the entire perimeter of the crankcase with a plastic or rubber mallet to make sure that both halves are closed completely together.

15. Install and tighten the 2 bolts (A, **Figure 110**) securing the crankcase halves together.

Spin the crankshaft and transmission shafts to make sure they rotate freely. If there is a slight amount of binding, tap on the end of all shafts with a plastic or rubber mallet.

Steps 16-21 relate only to 1977 and later models.

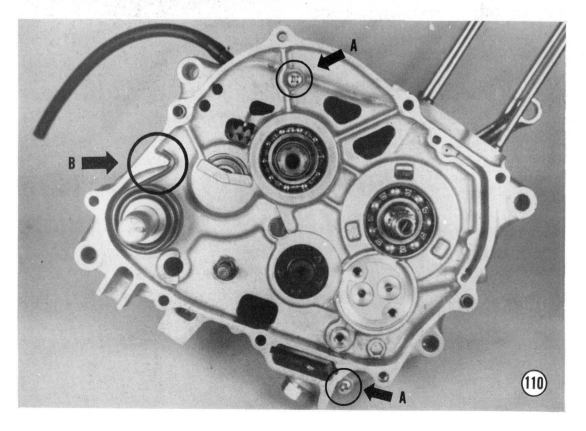

16. Install the kickstarter spring onto the spindle, inserting the short end in the hole in the spindle.

17. Install the spring spacer with the groove inserted over the short end of the kickstarter spring.

18. Hook the end of the kickstarter spring over the lug (B, **Figure 110**) on the crankcase.

19. Install the gearshift spindle (A, **Figure 111**) and return spring (B, **Figure 111**).

20. Install the cam plate (C, **Figure 111**).

> NOTE: *Check the function of the shift drum. Turn the shift drum with a 10mm socket on the cam bolt. Spin the transmission shafts by hand and shift the gears.*

21. Install the detent arm and spring (D, **Figure 111**).

Bearing Replacement

1. The bearings are lightly pressed into the crankcase halves (**Figure 112**). They may be driven out with a hammer and suitable size socket (**Figure 113**).

2. If the bearings are too tight, the crankcase halves will have to be heated. Place them in an oven and heat to 212°F (100°C). An easy way to check to see that it is at proper temperature is to drop tiny drops of water on the cases; if they sizzle and evaporate immediately, the temperature is correct.

3. Repeat Step 1 and remove the bearings — remember, the cases are still hot.

4. After removal of the bearings, thoroughly clean out the bearing recess in the crankcase.

5. Reheat the crankcase halves to the same temperature as in Step 2 and insert the bearings. They should fall right into place; if not, tap them in with a plastic mallet — very gently around the outer perimeter of the bearing. Make sure it completely seats.

TRANSMISSION

In order to gain access to the transmission components, it is necessary to split the crank-

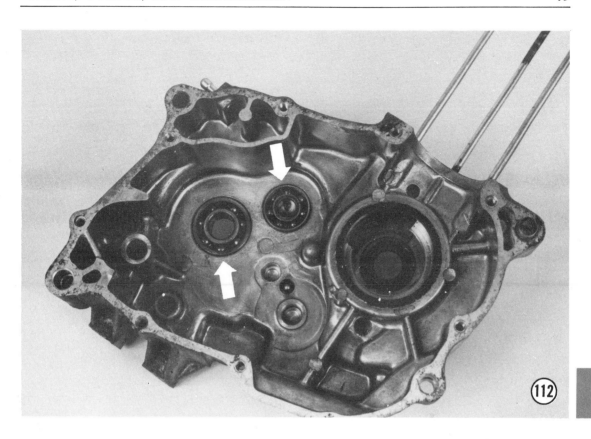

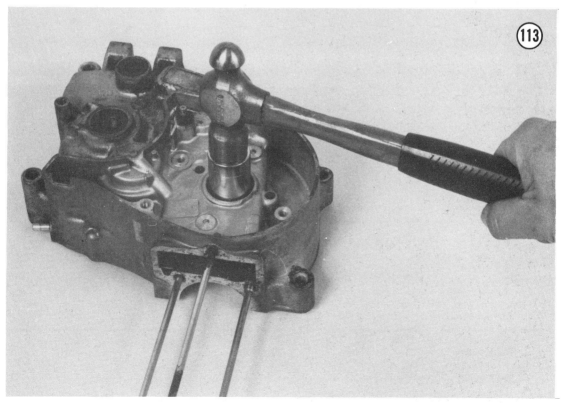

case as described under *Crankcase Disassembly* in this chapter.

Exploded-view drawings of the transmission are shown in **Figure 114** for 1975-1976 models and **Figure 115** for 1977 and later models. Refer to them for the following procedures.

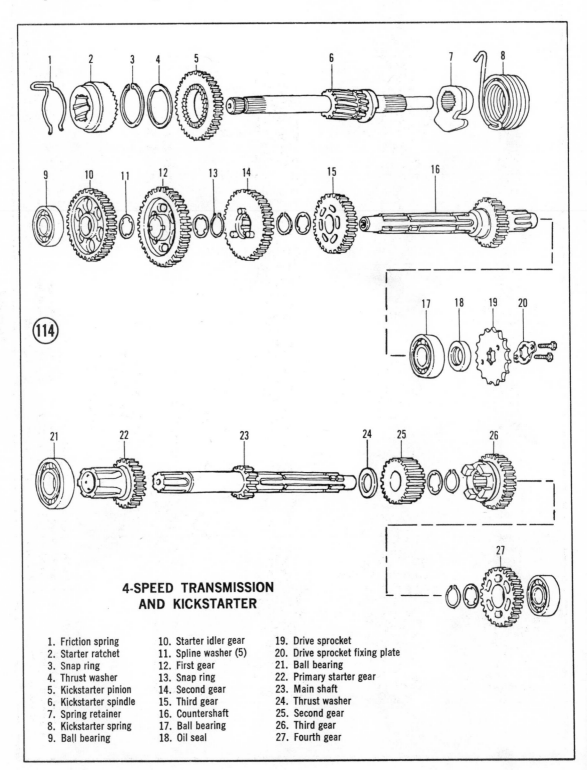

4-SPEED TRANSMISSION AND KICKSTARTER

1. Friction spring	10. Starter idler gear	19. Drive sprocket
2. Starter ratchet	11. Spline washer (5)	20. Drive sprocket fixing plate
3. Snap ring	12. First gear	21. Ball bearing
4. Thrust washer	13. Snap ring	22. Primary starter gear
5. Kickstarter pinion	14. Second gear	23. Main shaft
6. Kickstarter spindle	15. Third gear	24. Thrust washer
7. Spring retainer	16. Countershaft	25. Second gear
8. Kickstarter spring	17. Ball bearing	26. Third gear
9. Ball bearing	18. Oil seal	27. Fourth gear

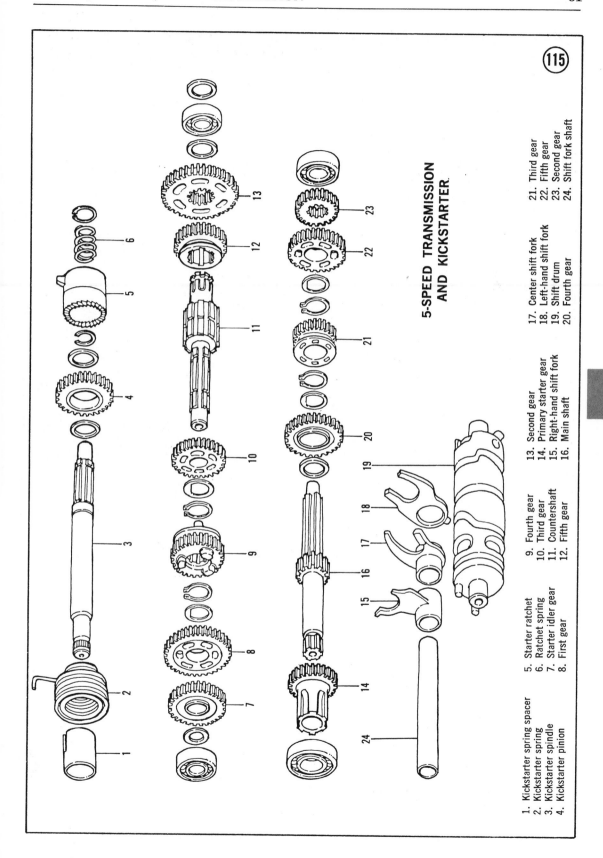

(115)

**5-SPEED TRANSMISSION
AND KICKSTARTER.**

1. Kickstarter spring spacer
2. Kickstarter spring
3. Kickstarter spindle
4. Kickstarter pinion
5. Starter ratchet
6. Ratchet spring
7. Starter idler gear
8. First gear
9. Fourth gear
10. Third gear
11. Countershaft
12. Fifth gear
13. Second gear
14. Primary starter gear
15. Right-hand shift fork
16. Main shaft
17. Center shift fork
18. Left-hand shift fork
19. Shift drum
20. Fourth gear
21. Third gear
22. Fifth gear
23. Second gear
24. Shift fork shaft

5

Mainshaft Disassembly/Assembly (1975-1976)

1. Remove the 4th gear (**Figure 116**).

2. Remove the spline washer, snap ring, and the 3rd gear (**Figure 117**).

3. Remove the snap ring, spline washer, and the 2nd gear (**Figure 118**).

4. Slide off the thrust washer (**Figure 119**).

5. Remove the primary starter gear (**Figure 120**).

6. Inspect all gears and parts as described under *Transmission and Kickstarter Inspection* in this chapter.

7. Assemble by reversing the removal steps. Refer to **Figure 121** for correct positioning of the gears. Make sure that all snap rings are correctly seated in the mainshaft grooves.

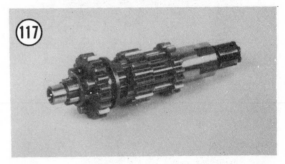

Countershaft Disassembly/Assembly (1975-1976)

1. Remove the primary starter idle gear (**Figure 122**).

2. Slide off the spline washer and 1st gear (**Figure 123**).

3. Remove the spline washer, snap ring, and the 2nd gear (**Figure 124**).

4. Remove the snap ring, spline washer, and the 3rd gear (**Figure 125**).

5. Inspect all gears and parts as described under *Transmission and Kickstarter Inspection* in this chapter.

6. Assemble by reversing the removal steps. Refer to **Figure 121** for correct positioning of the gears. Make sure that all snap rings are correctly seated in the countershaft grooves.

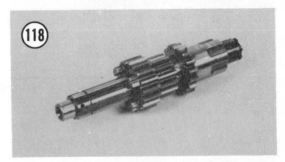

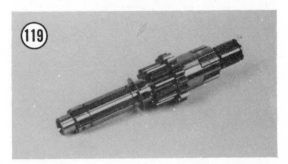

Kickstarter Disassembly/Assembly (1975-1976)

1. Slide off the kickstarter spring retainer and spring (**Figure 126**).

2. Remove the starter drive ratchet and friction spring (**Figure 127**).

3. Slide off the starter pinion gear (**Figure 128**).

4. Remove the snap ring and slide off the thrust washer.

5. Inspect all parts as described under *Transmission and Kickstarter Inspection* in this chapter.

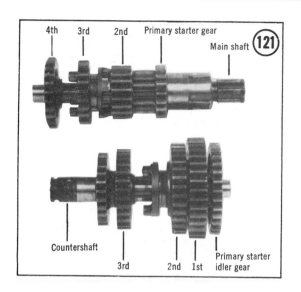

4th 3rd 2nd Primary starter gear

Main shaft

Countershaft

3rd 2nd 1st Primary starter idler gear

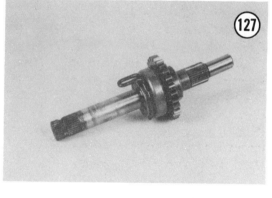

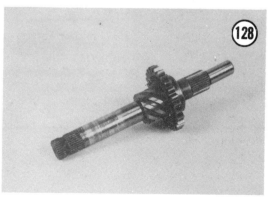

6. Assemble by reversing the disassembly steps. Make sure that the snap ring is correctly seated in the kickstarter shaft groove.

Mainshaft Disassembly/Assembly (1977 and Later)

1. Slide off the 2nd gear and 5th gear.
2. Remove the spline washer and snap ring.
3. Slide off 3rd gear.
4. Remove the snap ring and spline washer.
5. Slide off 4th gear and thrust washer.
6. Slide off the primary starter gear.
7. Inspect all gears and parts as described under *Transmission and Kickstarter Inspection* in this chapter.
8. Assemble by reversing the disassembly steps. Refer to **Figure 129** for correct positioning of

the gears. Make sure that all snap rings are correctly seated in the mainshaft grooves.

Countershaft Disassembly/Assembly (1977 and Later)

1. Slide off the thrust washer, 2nd gear, and the 5th gear.
2. Slide off the thrust washer, starter idle gear, and 1st gear.
3. Remove the spline washer and snap ring.
4. Slide off 4th gear.
5. Remove the snap ring and spline washer.
6. Slide off 3rd gear.
7. Inspect all gears and parts as described under *Transmission and Kickstarter Inspection* in this chapter.
8. Assemble by reversing the disassembly steps. Refer to **Figure 129** for correct positioning of

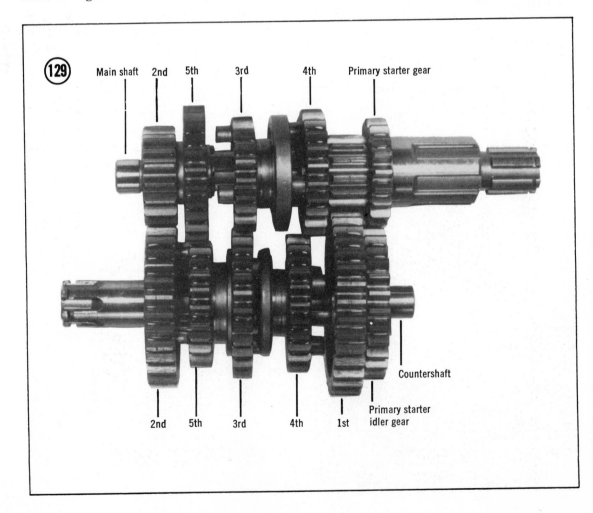

(129) Main shaft   2nd   5th   3rd   4th   Primary starter gear

Countershaft

2nd   5th   3rd   4th   1st   Primary starter idler gear

the gears. Make sure that all snap rings are correctly seated in the countershaft grooves.

Kickstarter Disassembly/Assembly (1977 and Later)

1. Remove the snap ring and ratchet spring.

2. Slide off the starter ratchet.

3. Remove the 2 washers and kickstarter pinion gear.

4. Slide off the thrust washer.

5. Inspect all parts as described under *Transmission and Kickstarter Inspection* in this chapter.

6. Assemble by reversing the disassembly steps. Make sure that the snap ring is correctly seated in the kickstarter shaft groove.

Transmission and Kickstarter Inspection (All Models)

1. Clean all parts in cleaning solvent and thoroughly dry.

2. Check each gear for excessive wear and for chipped or missing teeth. Make sure the lugs on ends of gears are in good condition.

3. Make sure that all gears slide smoothly on their respective shaft splines.

4. Check that the kickstarter drive ratchet operates properly.

5. Check the bearings in the crankcase halves (**Figure 130**). Make sure they operate smoothly with no signs of wear or damage.

GEARSHIFT DRUM AND FORKS

Refer to **Figure 131** for this procedure. The parts shown are from a 1975-1976 model. On 1977 and later models there is an additional shift fork and the gear shift drum configuration is a little different. Inspection is basically the same.

In order to gain access to the gear shift drum and shift forks, it is necessary to split the crankcase as described under *Crankcase Disassembly* in this chapter.

Inspection

1. Wash all parts in cleaning solvent and thoroughly dry.

2. Measure the inside diameter of the shift forks with an inside micrometer (**Figure 132**). Replace the ones worn beyond the wear limits given in **Table 1**.

3. Measure the width of the gearshift fingers with a micrometer (**Figure 133**). Replace the ones worn beyond the wear limit in **Table 1**.

4. Measure the outside diameter of the shift fork shaft with a micrometer. Replace if worn beyond the wear limit given in **Table 1**.

5

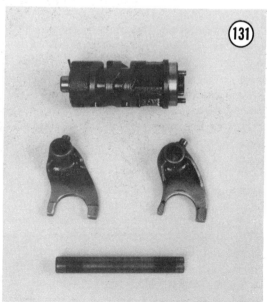

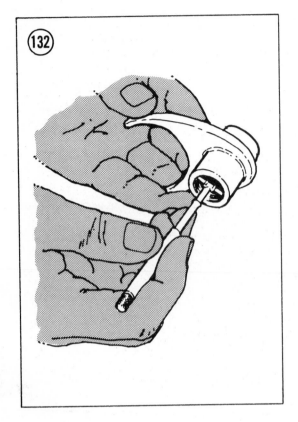

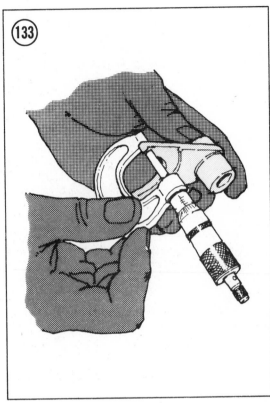

5. Check that the grooves in the shift drum are in good condition and that the drum rotates freely in the bearing surfaces in the crankcase halves.

BREAK-IN

Following cylinder servicing (boring, honing, new rings, etc.) and major lower end work, the engine should be broken in just as though it were new. The performance and service life of the engine depend greatly on a careful and sensible break-in.

For the first 500 miles, no more than one-third throttle should be used and speed should be varied as much as possible within the one-third throttle limit. Prolonged, steady running at one speed, no matter how moderate, is to be avoided, as is hard acceleration.

Following the 500-mile service, increasingly more throttle can be used but full throttle should not be used until the motorcycle has covered at least 1,000 miles and then it should be limited to short bursts until 1,500 miles have been logged.

The mono-grade oils recommended for break-in and normal use provide a better bedding pattern for rings and cylinders than do multi-grade oils. As a result, piston ring and cylinder bore life are greatly increased. During this period, oil consumption will be higher than normal. It is therefore important to frequently check and correct the oil level. At no time, during break-in or later, should the oil level be allowed to drop below the bottom line on the dipstick; if the oil level is low, the oil will become overheated, resulting in insufficient lubrication and increased wear.

500-Mile Service

It is essential that the oil and filter be changed after the first 500 miles. In addition, it is a good idea to change the oil and filter at the completion of break-in (about 1,500 miles) to ensure that all of the particles produced during break-in are removed from the lubrication system. The small added expense may be considered a smart investment that will pay off in increased engine life.

Table 1   ENGINE SPECIFICATIONS

Item	Specification (new)	Wear Limit
Cam height		
Intake	1.0896-1.0972 in. (27.677-27.717mm)	1.0827 in. (27.5mm)
Exhaust	1.0833-1.0861 in. (27.540-27.586mm)	1.0772 in. (27.36mm)
Rocker arm to shaft clearance	0.0005-0.0015 in. (0.013-0.037mm)	0.0039 in. (0.1mm)
Valve stem outer diameter		
Intake	0.2146-0.2152 in. (5.450-5.465mm)	0.2134 in. (5.42mm)
Exhaust	0.2138-0.2144 in. (5.430-5.445mm)	0.2126 in. (5.40mm)
Valve to valve guide clearance		
Intake	0.0004-0.0014 in. (0.01-0.035mm)	0.0031 in. (0.078mm)
Exhaust	0.0012-0.0022 in. (0.03-0.055mm)	0.0039 in. (0.1mm)
Valve spring free length		
Inner	1.1043 in. (28.05mm)	1.0630 in. (27.0mm)
Outer	1.3307 in. (33.8mm)	1.2874 in. (32.7mm)
Cylinder bore	1.8504-1.8508 in. (47.0-47.01mm)	1.8543 in. (47.1mm)
Piston skirt outer diameter	1.8492-1.8500 in. (46.97-46.99mm)	1.8425 in. (46.80mm)
Piston wrist pin bore	0.5119-0.5121 in. (13.002-13.008mm)	0.5142 in. (13.06mm)
Piston wrist pin outer diameter	0.5116-0.5118 in. (12.994-13.00mm)	0.5079 in. (12.9mm)
Piston ring side clearance		
Top and second ring	0.0006-0.0018 in. (0.015-0.045mm)	0.0059 in. (0.15mm)
Oil ring	0	—
Piston ring end gap		
Top and second ring	0.0059-0.0138 in. (0.15-0.35mm)	0.0197 in. (0.5mm)
Oil ring	0.0118-0.0354 in. (0.3-0.9mm)	—
Oil pump		
Outer rotor to body clearance	0.0059 in. (0.15mm)	0.0079 in. (0.2mm)
Inner to outer rotor clearance	0.0059 in. (0.15mm)	0.0079 in. (0.2mm)
Clutch friction disc thickness	0.1102-0.1142 in. (2.8-2.9mm)	0.0984 in. (2.5mm)
Clutch spring free length	1.0748 in. (27.3mm)	0.9961 in. (25.3mm)
Gear shift fork width	0.1941-0.1969 in. (4.93-5.0mm)	0.1772 in. (4.5mm)
Gear shift fork inner diameter	0.4724-0.4731 in. (12.00-12.018mm)	0.4726 in. (12.05mm)
Gear shift fork shaft outer diameter	0.4715-0.4722 in. (11.976-11.994mm)	0.4685 in. (11.9mm)
Gear shift fork guide to drum groove clearance	0.0020-0.0079 in. (0.05-0.2mm)	0.0118 in. (0.3mm)

5

Table 2   ENGINE TORQUE VALUES

Item	Ft.-lb.	N•m
Crankcase and engine side covers	5-9	7-12
Cam cover	6-9	8-12
Camshaft holder	6-9	8-12
Intake manifold	6-9	8-12
Magneto rotor	22-28	30-38
Oil filter rotor	25-33	34-45
Valve clearance adjust nut	5-8	7-11
Cam sprocket bolts	7-12	9-16
Engine oil drain plug	15-22	20-30

CHAPTER SIX

FUEL, IGNITION, AND EXHAUST SYSTEMS

The fuel system consists of the fuel tank, fuel shutoff valve, fuel line, carburetor, and air filter.

CARBURETOR

The carburetor used on the XR75 (**Figure 1**) utilizes an integral float bowl beneath the cable-actuated throttle slide. The amount of air is controlled by the cylindrical slide while the amount of fuel that passes from the float chamber to the engine is controlled by a main jet, a needle jet, and a tapered needle that operates within the needle jet. Various adjustments can be made to the carburetion mixture by substituting different jets and needles, or by varying the position of the needle in the throttle slide.

Basic Principles

Understanding the function of the carburetor will enable carburetor troubles to be pinpointed and rectified in a shorter time. Unfortunately, the carburetor is very accessible and is often the first engine component to be tinkered with when running difficulties arise. Therefore, a basic understanding of how it works and how to properly adjust it may save unnecessary effort and expense.

The carburetor is a device that mixes air and fuel in the proper proportion desired by the engine. Should this ratio of fuel to air (ideal is approximately 14 parts air to one part fuel) change in any way, the fuel/air mixture changes. If there is too much air, the mixture is said to be "lean". If there is too much fuel, the mixture is considered "rich".

Fuel for the carburetor is stored in the float bowl underneath the main body. The amount of fuel that is stored in the bowl is controlled by the float system which shuts off the supply of fuel from the tank at a predetermined level. This is called the float level. As the fuel pours into the float bowl, the buoyant floats rise. As they reach the point of the desired float level, the movement of the floats actuates the needle and seat. The needle and seat shut off the flow of fuel. As the supply of fuel in the float bowl decreases, the floats lower opening the needle and seat, and more fuel is allowed to flow into the float bowl. This happens continuously as the machine is in use, providing a constant supply of fuel to the engine.

In addition to supplying the engine the needed ideal fuel mixture, the carburetor must also supply varying amounts for the particular conditions under which the engine is being run.

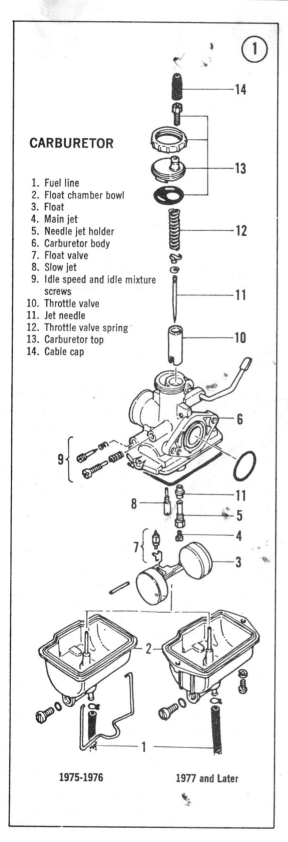

CARBURETOR

1. Fuel line
2. Float chamber bowl
3. Float
4. Main jet
5. Needle jet holder
6. Carburetor body
7. Float valve
8. Slow jet
9. Idle speed and idle mixture screws
10. Throttle valve
11. Jet needle
12. Throttle valve spring
13. Carburetor top
14. Cable cap

1975-1976   1977 and Later

At very low engine speeds, the carburetor utilizes an idle system to provide small quantities required. At medium engine speeds, the main jet supply is metered by a tapered needle that is connected directly to the throttle slide that controls the amount of air. As the throttle is opened, the tapered needle moves in the needle jet; the taper allows increasing amounts of fuel to be supplied as the throttle and the needle are moved. Substituting needles with different degrees of taper allows for differing amounts of fuel to be supplied at given throttle openings.

Once the engine is operated at or near maximum speeds, the fuel supply becomes the sole job of the main jet. The throttle slide allows the maximum amount of air to pass into the engine and has raised the needle well clear of any restriction in the needle jet. The air passing through the carburetor bore draws fuel directly from the float bowl up through the main jet. Changes in the size of the main jet will determine the amount of fuel.

Idle Speed and Mixture Adjustment

Idle speed should be set at 1,400 rpm. If a tachometer is not available, set the idle to the lowest speed that allows the engine to continue to run at all times. Even when hot, the engine should idle once the clutch is disengaged and the transmission is placed in neutral.

The engine should be at normal operating temperature prior to adjusting the carburetor.

1. Set the idle speed to 1,400 rpm with the idle speed screw (A, **Figure 2**).

2. Screw the idle mixture screw (B, **Figure 2**) carefully in until it seats. Back-out the screw 1¼ turns.

CAUTION
*Do not screw the idle mixture screw in
tight or the seat in the carburetor will be
damaged.*

3. Turn the idle mixture screw counterclockwise until the engine misses or idle speed increases. Note the position of the screw.

4. Turn the idle mixture screw clockwise until the engine misses or the idle speed decreases. Note the position of the screw.

5. Set the idle mixture screw midway between the 2 points.

6. Readjust the idle speed to 1,400 rpm.

Needle Adjustments

The needle position can be changed to affect the fuel/air mixture during medium throttle openings.

1. Remove the top of the carburetor and remove the slide assembly (**Figure 3**).

2. Compress the slide spring against the carburetor top. This will free the cable in the bottom of the throttle slide.

3. Remove the slide.

4. Remove the needle from the slide and note the position of the needle retaining clip (**Figure 4**).

5. Raising the needle will richen the mixture during mid-throttle openings, while lowering it will lean the mixture. The standard setting is the second groove from the top of the needle (**Figure 4**).

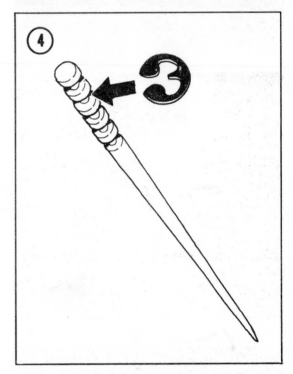

Float Level Adjustment

The float level can be adjusted by bending the small tab on the float bracket where it contacts the needle and seat. The float level height can be checked as in **Figure 5**. When the small tab is just touching the needle portion of the needle and seat, the dimension from the bottom of the groove of the carburetor mating surface to the bottom of the float should be 0.827 in. (21mm) on 1975 models and 0.7874 in. (20mm) on 1976 and later models.

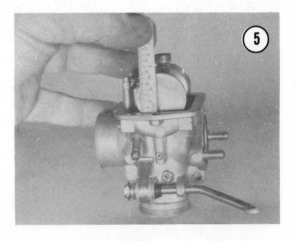

Removal/Installation

1. Remove the side cover.

2. Remove the spring clip securing the air filter intake tube to the carburetor (**Figure 6**). Slip the tube off the carburetor intake.

3. Unscrew the top of the carburetor and remove the carburetor top, throttle slide, and slide spring (**Figure 3**).

4. Remove the fuel line where it enters the float bowl (**Figure 7**).

5. On 1977 and later models, remove the two 6mm nuts securing the carburetor to the intake manifold (**Figure 8**). On 1975-1976 models, the carburetor is secured to the intake manifold by a spring clip. Remove the clip.

6. Remove the carburetor.

7. Disconnect the throttle cable from the throttle slide.

8. Installation is the reverse of these steps. However, care should be taken in the following areas.

9. Be sure that the throttle cable is seated in the recess provided in the throttle slide.

10. When installing the throttle slide, be sure that the slot in the slide engages the pin in the carburetor body. The "cutaway" side of the slide should face the air filter when assembled.

Disassembly/Assembly

1. Remove the idle speed screw and spring (A, **Figure 9**).

2. Remove the idle mixture screw and spring (B, **Figure 9**).

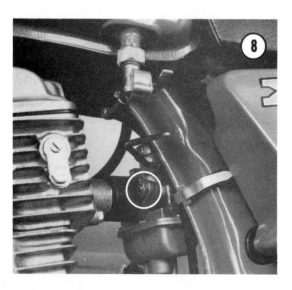

A. Idle speed
B. Idle mixture

6

3. Remove the float bowl. On 1975-1976 models, the bowl is secured to the float chamber with a spring clip; on 1977 and later models it is held with 2 screws. See **Figure 10**.

4. Press out the float pivot pin with a small screwdriver or pointed scribe (**Figure 11**).

5. Remove the float assembly (**Figure 12**).

6. Remove the main jet (A, **Figure 13**).

7. Remove the needle jet holder (A, **Figure 13**); it is located under the main jet. The needle jet is held in place by the threaded needle jet and can be removed once the holder is removed.

8. Remove the slow jet (B, **Figure 13**).

9. On 1975-1976 models, lift the needle out of the seat. On 1977 and later models, remove the clip securing the needle to the float.

10. Remove the needle seat (C, **Figure 13**).

11. Remove the nut securing the choke lever to the carburetor body (**Figure 14**). Remove the lever.

12. Slide the choke assembly out of the top of the carburetor body.

13. Assemble by reversing the disassembly steps. Check to make sure of the following steps.

14. On 1977 and later models, the wire clip attaching the needle portion of the needle and seat to the float assembly is easily lost; be sure it is installed.

15. Make sure the gasket on the float bowl is in good condition. On 1975-1976 models, make sure the cork gasket is completely seated in the carburetor body.

Cleaning and Inspection

1. Clean all parts, except rubber or plastic parts, in a good grade of carburetor cleaner. Follow the manufacturer's instructions for correct soak time (usually about ½ hour).

2. Blow compressed air through all passages to make sure that they are clean and free of obstructions. *Do not* use a piece of wire to clean the jets as minor gouges in a jet can alter the flow rate and upset the fuel/air mixture.

3. Examine the tips of all adjustment screws for scoring or grooves. If there is any sign of damage, replace the screw.

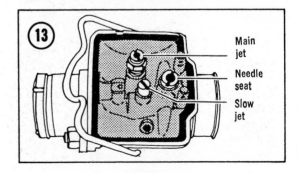

Main jet

Needle seat

Slow jet

⑭

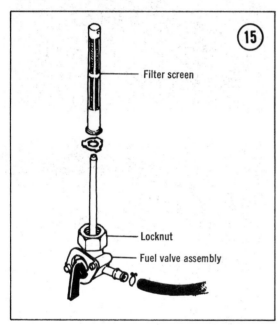

⑮

Filter screen

Locknut

Fuel valve assembly

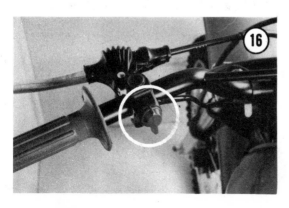

⑯

4. Shake the float assembly to see if any fuel has found its way into either float. If it has, replace the float assembly.

5. Examine the needle and seat for signs of grooving that might allow leakage.

6. Check all gaskets for proper seal.

FUEL SHUTOFF VALVE

Removal/Installation

1. Turn the fuel shutoff valve to the OFF position and remove the flexible fuel line to the carburetor.

2. Place the loose end into a clean, sealable metal container. This fuel can be reused if it is kept clean.

3. Open the valve to the RESERVE position and remove the fuel fill cap. This will allow air to enter the tank and speed up the flow of fuel. Drain the tank completely.

4. Remove the fuel shutoff valve by unscrewing the locknut from the tank.

5. After removing the valve, insert a corner of a clean shop rag into the opening of the tank to stop the dribbling of fuel onto the engine and frame.

6. Remove the fuel filter from the valve (**Figure 15**). Clean it with a medium soft toothbrush and blow with compressed air. Replace it if defective.

7. Install by reversing the removal steps. Do not forget the gasket.

IGNITION SYSTEM

The ignition system on the XR75 is very basic, consisting of a magneto mounted on the engine, an ignition coil mounted beneath the fuel tank that connects directly with the spark plug, and a handlebar-mounted ignition (on-off) switch (**Figure 16**).

If ignition malfunction is suspected, remove the spark plug and perform the following checks:

1. Place the spark plug in the spark plug cap and hold the metal portion of the plug against the cylinder head (**Figure 17**).

2. Turn the ignition switch to the ON position and turn the engine over by using the kickstarter. The plug should spark.

6

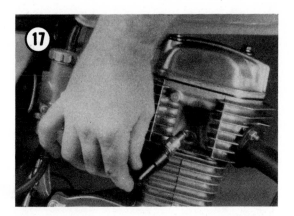

3. If there is no spark, replace the plug with a new one and repeat the procedure.

4. If there is still no spark at the plug, the fault lies in the wiring, the ignition coil or the magneto.

5. Check the fuse and the wiring and repeat the test procedure.

6. Remove the left-hand engine cover and inspect the magneto assembly. Align the "F" mark on the flywheel with the pointer on the engine and view the contact points through the hole provided in the flywheel. See **Figure 18** for 1975-1976 models and **Figure 19** for 1977 and later models.

7. Check the point gap with a feeler gauge. It should be 0.012-0.016 in. (0.3-0.4mm).

8. If the point gap is out of the allowable tolerance, it must be adjusted and re-checked or the points replaced if they cannot be adjusted to this specification. Refer to *Breaker Contact Points Replacement* in Chapter Four.

9. To adjust the point gap, loosen the contact breaker point attachment screw (A, **Figure 20**) and insert a screwdriver between the adjusting notches (B, **Figure 20**) and turn slightly to open or close the point gap.

10. If the preceding checks and adjustments do not rectify the problem, the cause lies in either the capacitor or the ignition coil. Both components require special testing equipment and should be taken to a Honda dealer who has the proper test equipment.

Ignition Timing

Refer to *Breaker Point Adjustment and Magneto Timing* in Chapter Four.

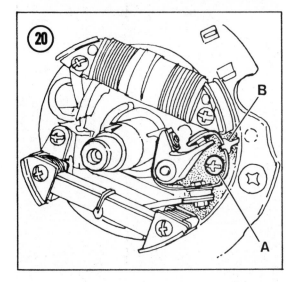

EXHAUST SYSTEM

The only maintenance on the exhaust system is to check that the gasket on the cylinder head is in good condition and to remove carbon buildup in the muffler interior.

Removal/Installation

1. Loosen the 2 nuts securing the exhaust pipe to the cylinder head **(Figure 21)**.

2. Loosen and remove the nut **(Figure 22)** securing the muffler to the rear swing arm pivot bolt.

3. Remove the 2 nuts on the cylinder head studs **(Figure 21)** and remove the exhaust pipe/muffler assembly.

4. Install by reversing the removal steps. After fitting the system back in place, tighten the 2 nuts securing the exhaust pipe to the cylinder head *first* then the nut on the rear swing arm pivot bolt.

Carbon Removal and Inspection

Scrape carbon from all accessible areas with a screwdriver blade. Clean out the inside of the exhaust pipe by running a piece of used drive chain through it. Another way is to chuck a length of wire cable, with one end frayed, in an electric drill. Run it through a couple of times. Blow out all loose carbon deposits with compressed air.

Inspect the muffler body and exhaust pipe to make sure they are not dented or cracked. Straighten out or replace.

6

CHAPTER SEVEN

WHEELS AND BRAKES

FRONT WHEEL

Removal/Installation

1. Support the motorcycle with the front wheel elevated.

2. Remove the cotter pin securing the axle nut (**Figure 1**).

3. Loosen the axle nut and remove it (**Figure 2**).

4. Support the wheel with one hand while removing the axle with the other. This will free the wheel from the fork assembly (**Figure 3**).

5. Move the wheel forward of the fork tube and slip the brake plate assembly free from the

brake drum. The brake plate assembly will now be held only by the brake cable.

6. Remove the cotter pin in the brake arm and free the brake cable from the brake plate.

7. Install by reversing the removal steps.

8. Tighten the axle nut to 29-40 ft.-lb. (39-54 N•m) and install a *new* cotter pin. Bend the ends over completely.

REAR WHEEL

Removal/Installation

1. Support the motorcycle with the rear wheel elevated.

2. Remove the brake rod adjusting nut and the cotter pin and bolt securing the anchor arm (A, **Figure 4**).

3. Loosen the chain adjusting nut on each side of the axle (B, **Figure 4**).

4. Remove the cotter pin securing the axle nut.

5. Remove the axle nut (**Figure 4**).

6. Slide the wheel forward and lift the chain off the rear sprocket.

7. Remove the axle and the rear wheel.

8. Install by reversing the removal steps.

9. Tighten the axle nut to 29-40 ft.-lb. (39-54 N•m) and install a *new* cotter pin. Bend the ends over completely.

Wheel Inspection

Refer to **Figures 5 and 6** for this procedure.

1. Inspect all parts for wear.

2. Check the wheel bearings for roughness.

3. Check the wheel spokes for proper tension. Each should be tightened to 1.1-1.5 ft.-lb. (1.5-2.0 N•m).

4. Check the brake drum surface for scratches or gouges that might reduce the braking effectiveness.

> NOTE: *Steps 5 and 6 are for rear wheel only.*

5. Check the sprocket teeth for wear (**Figure 7**).

6. Check the drive chain for wear or tight links. If necessary, remove the chain, clean and lubricate it as described under *Drive Chain Cleaning and Lubrication* in this chapter.

7

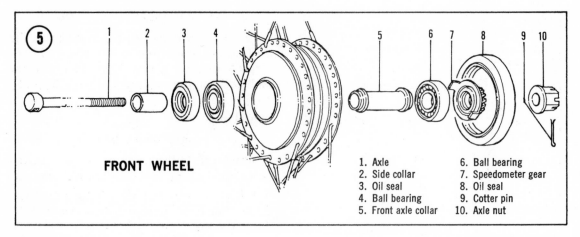

FRONT WHEEL

1. Axle
2. Side collar
3. Oil seal
4. Ball bearing
5. Front axle collar
6. Ball bearing
7. Speedometer gear
8. Oil seal
9. Cotter pin
10. Axle nut

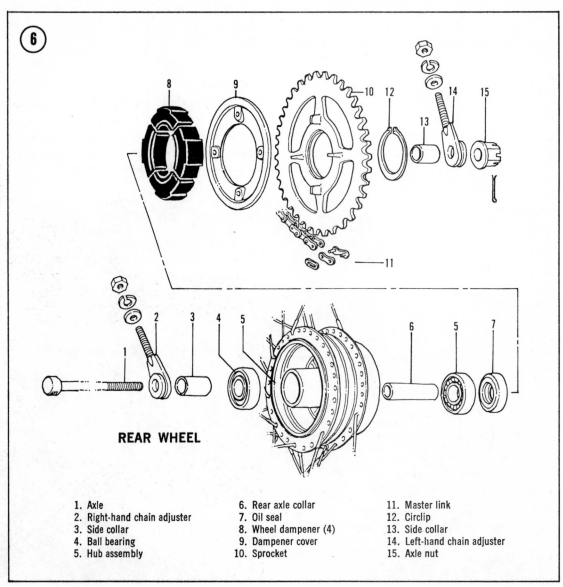

REAR WHEEL

1. Axle
2. Right-hand chain adjuster
3. Side collar
4. Ball bearing
5. Hub assembly
6. Rear axle collar
7. Oil seal
8. Wheel dampener (4)
9. Dampener cover
10. Sprocket
11. Master link
12. Circlip
13. Side collar
14. Left-hand chain adjuster
15. Axle nut

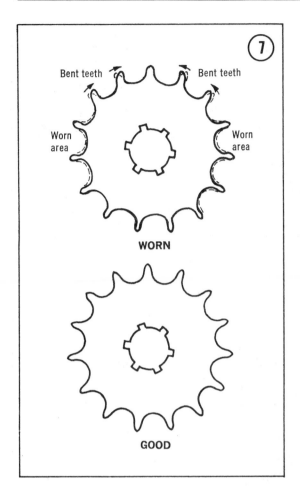

Bent teeth   Bent teeth

Worn
area

Worn
area

WORN

GOOD

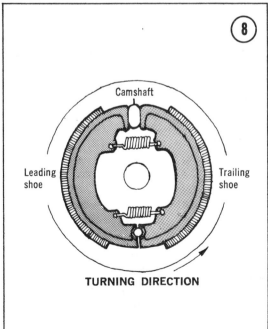

Camshaft

Leading
shoe

Trailing
shoe

TURNING DIRECTION

BRAKES

Figure 8 illustrates the major parts of the brakes. Squeezing the brake lever on the handlebar rotates the cam, which in turn forces the brake shoes out into contact with the brake drum.

BRAKE CABLE

Brake cable adjustment should be checked periodically as the cables stretch out with use and increase brake lever free play. Free play is the distance that the brake lever travels between the released position and the point when the brake shoes come in contact with the drum. This should be adjusted so that the tip of the brake lever moves about 0.8 in. (20mm) before the brakes make contact (**Figure 9**).

Adjustment

1. Loosen the locknut (A) and turn the adjusting barrel (B) *clockwise* to reduce slack in the cable (**Figure 10**).

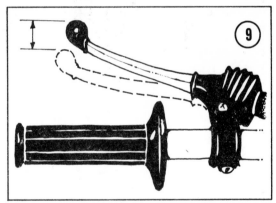

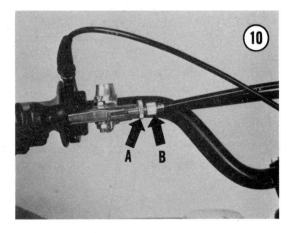

A   B

7

2. If the cable has stretched enough that this adjustment is not enough, the cable will have to be adjusted at the brake plate.

3. Screw the adjusting barrel (B) all the way in toward the handgrip.

4. At the brake plate, loosen the locknut (A) and turn the adjustment nut (B) on the end of the outer cable housing toward the end of the housing (**Figure 11**). Tighten the locknut. This will take out the necessary slack.

> NOTE: *If proper adjustment cannot be achieved by using both of these methods, the cable will have to be replaced. See Brake Cable Removal/ Installation in this chapter.*

Removal/Installation

In time, the cable will stretch to the point where it is no longer useful and will have to be replaced.

1. Remove the locknut (A) at the brake plate (**Figure 11**).

2. Push up on the brake arm and slip the end of the cable out. Pull up on the outer cable housing to remove the threaded end from the brake plate.

> NOTE: *On rear wheel, it is necessary to remove brake arm return spring prior to removal of cable.*

3. Pull the hand lever all the way back to the grip, remove the cable nipple holder and remove the cable from the lever.

4. Remove the cable from the frame.

> NOTE: *Prior to removal of the cable, make a drawing of the routing of the cable through the frame. It is very easy to forget how it was once it has been removed. Replace it exactly as it was, avoiding any sharp turns.*

5. Install by reversing the removal steps, adjusting the brakes as described under *Brake Cable Adjustment* in this chapter.

BRAKE LINING

Inspection

The brake linings should be replaced if worn within $\frac{5}{64}$ in. (2mm) of the metal shoe table (**Figure 12**). This is measured at the thinnest part.

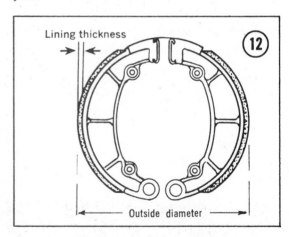

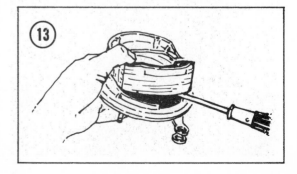

Removal/Installation

1. Remove front and/or rear wheel as described under *Front or Rear Wheel Removal/Installation* this chapter.

2. Pull the brake assembly off the hub.

3. Remove the brake shoe assembly, including the return springs from the brake plate. Pry each shoe from the brake plate **(Figure 13)** using a screwdriver or similar tool.

4. Inspect the linings for any traces of oil or grease. If they are contaminated, they should be replaced. Dirt embedded in the linings may be removed with a wire brush.

5. If the existing linings are to be reinstalled, roughen them up slightly with fine emery cloth. Be sure to thoroughly wipe all residue from the linings.

6. Check the cam and pivot pin for wear and corrosion. Clean off any corrosion with fine emery cloth. Check that the cam rotates freely. If cam or pivot pin is worn, the brake plate should be replaced.

7. Inspect the brake return springs for wear. If they are stretched they will not fully retract the brake shoes and they will drag and wear out prematurely. Replace if necessary.

8. Install by reversing the removal steps. Apply a light coat of grease to the cam and pivot pin. Avoid getting any grease on the brake plate where the linings may come in contact with it. Hold the shoes in a V-formation with the springs attached and snap them in place on the brake plate.

> NOTE: *If new linings are being installed, file off the leading edge of each shoe a little (Figure 14) so that the brakes will not grab when applied.*

BRAKE DRUM

Removal/Installation/Inspection

1. Remove front and/or rear wheel as described under *Front or Rear Wheel Removal/Installation* in this chapter.

2. Pull the brake assembly out of hub.

3. Inspect the drum for deep grooves, roughness, or scoring **(Figure 15)**. Replace if necessary.

4. Roughen up the surface of the drum with fine emery paper. Blow out all residue with compressed air.

5. Measure the inside diameter of the brake drum **(Figure 16)**. Nominal size is 4.3228-

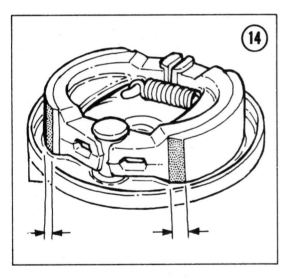

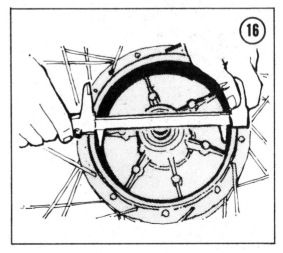

4.3386 in. (109.8-110.2mm). If this measurement is 4.370 in. (111mm) or more, the drum must be replaced.

6. Install by reversing the removal steps.

DRIVE CHAIN

Inspection

The chain is one of the most severely stressed parts of the bike. Inspect the chain carefully whenever it is removed for cleaning. Pay particular attention to cracks in the rollers and pin and link plates (**Figure 17**). Wear on these parts will cause the chain to stretch. As a quick check of chain wear, refer to **Figure 18**. Replace the chain if it can be pulled away from the rear sprocket by more than ½ the length of a link.

Cleaning and Lubrication

Chain removal is accomplished by removing the master link (**Figure 19**).

1. Remove the master link outer clip by prying it off with a thin bladed screwdriver.

2. Remove the outside plate and push the inside plate, complete with pins, out through the back of the chain.

3. Remove chain and soak it in cleaning solvent for about 30 minutes, to remove dirt, grease, and old chain oil. Move it around and flex it during this period so that dirt between the pins and rollers may work its way out.

4. Scrub rollers and side plates with a stiff brush, then rinse in clean solvent to carry away loosened dirt.

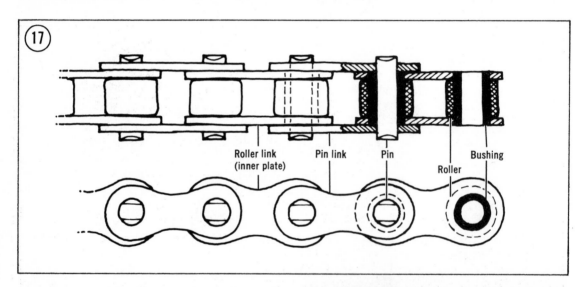

Roller link (inner plate) Pin link Pin Roller Bushing

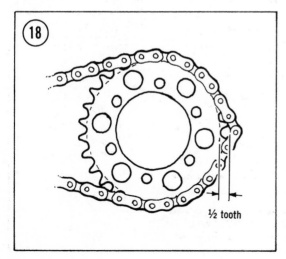

½ tooth

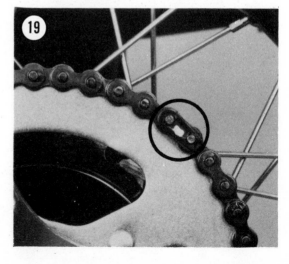

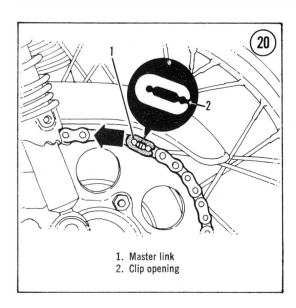

1. Master link
2. Clip opening

5. Hang chain and allow to dry thoroughly.

6. Lubricate chain with a good grade of commercial chain lubricant. Follow the lubricant manufacturer's application instructions.

7. Install by reversing the removal steps. Use a new master link clip and install it with the opening facing the opposite direction of chain travel (**Figure 20**). Incorrect installation will result in the loss of the clip and may result in chain breakage.

TIRES AND TUBES

Tire Removal

Refer to **Figure 21** for this procedure. Always leave the locknuts on the axle to protect the threads during tire removal/installation.

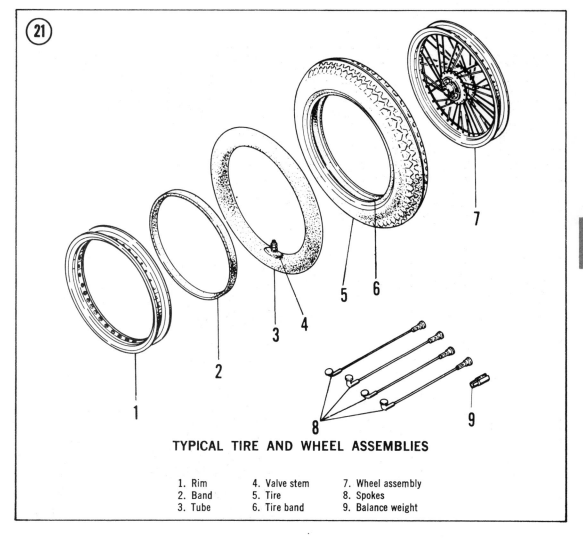

TYPICAL TIRE AND WHEEL ASSEMBLIES

1. Rim	4. Valve stem	7. Wheel assembly
2. Band	5. Tire	8. Spokes
3. Tube	6. Tire band	9. Balance weight

7

1. Unscrew the valve core from the valve stem with a special tool (**Figure 22**) and deflate tire.

2. Press the entire bead on both sides of the tire away from the rim and into center of the rim.

3. Lubricate the beads with soapy water.

4. Insert a tire iron under the top bead next to the valve. Force the bead on the opposite side of the tire into the center of the rim and pry the bead over the rim with the tire iron (**Figure 23**).

5. Insert a second tire iron next to the first to hold the bead over the rim. Then work around the tire with the first tire iron, prying the bead over the rim (**Figure 24**). Be careful not to pinch the inner tube with the tire irons.

6. Remove the valve from the hole in the rim and remove the tube from the tire.

> NOTE: *Step 7 is required only if it is necessary to completely remove tire from rim, such as for tire replacement.*

7. Insert a tire iron between the back bead and the side of the rim that the top bead was pried over (**Figure 25**). Force the bead on the opposite side from the tire iron into the center of the rim. Pry the back bead off the rim working around as with the first.

Tube Inspection

1. Install the valve core into the valve stem and inflate the tube slightly. Do not overinflate.

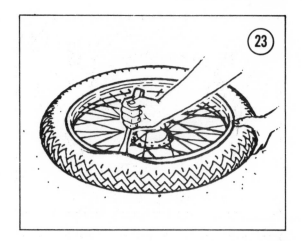

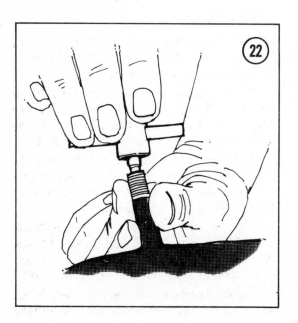

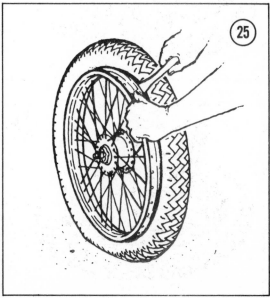

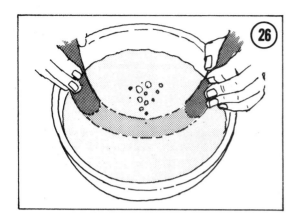

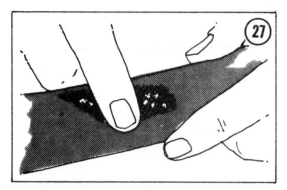

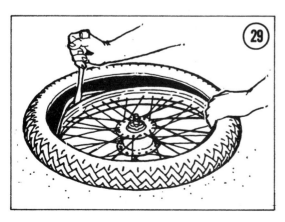

2. Immerse the tube in water a section at a time. See **Figure 26**. Look carefully for bubbles indicating a hole. Mark each hole and continue checking until you are certain that all holes are discovered and marked. Also make sure that the valve core is not leaking; tighten it if necessary.

> NOTE: *If you do not have enough water to immerse sections of the tube, try running your hand over the tube slowly and very close to the surface. If your hand is damp, it works even better. If you suspect a hole anywhere, apply some saliva to the area to verify it (**Figure 27**).*

3. Apply a patch using either the hot or cold patch techniques described under *Tire Repairs* in this chapter.

4. Dust the patch area with talcum powder to prevent it from sticking to the tire.

5. Carefully check inside the tire casing for glass particles, nails, or other objects which may have damaged the tube. If inside of tire is split, apply a patch to the area to prevent it from pinching and damaging the tube again.

6. Check the inside of the rim. Make sure the rim band is in place and no spoke ends protrude which could puncture the tube.

7. Deflate the tube prior to installation in the tire.

Tire Installation

1. Inflate the tube just enough to round it out. Too much air will make installation difficult.

2. Place the tube inside the tire.

3. Place back side of the tire into center of rim and insert the valve stem through the rim hole (**Figure 28**). The lower bead should go into the center of the rim with the upper bead outside it.

4. Starting opposite the valve stem, press the lower bead into the rim center working around the tire in both directions. Use a tire iron for the last few inches of bead (**Figure 29**).

5. Press the upper bead into the rim opposite the valve (**Figure 30**) and work around the tire in both directions with your hands. Use a tire iron for the last few inches of bead (**Figure 31**).

6. Wiggle the valve to be sure the tube is not under the bead. Set the valve squarely in its hole

7

before screwing in the valve nut to hold it against the rim.

7. Check the bead on both sides of the tire for even fit around the rim. Inflate the tire slowly to seat the beads in the rim. It may be necessary to bounce the tire to complete the seating. Inflate to correct pressure; front tire 17 psi (1.2 kg/cm) and rear tire 20 psi (1.4 kg/cm).

TIRE REPAIRS

Tire/tube damage will eventually strike even the most careful rider. Repair is fairly simple on all tires.

Tire Repair Kits

Tire repair kits can be purchased from motorcycles dealers and some auto supply stores. When buying, specify that the kit you want is for motorcycle tires. There are two types of tire repair kits:

    a. Hot patch

    b. Cold patch

Hot patches are strongest because they actually vulcanize to the tube, becoming part of it. The repair kit for hot patching is bulkier and heavier than cold patch kits, therefore, hot patch kits are more suited for home repairs.

Cold patches are not vulcanized to the tube, they are simply glued to it. Though not as strong as hot patches, cold patches are still very durable. Cold patch kits are less bulky than hot and more easily applied under adverse conditions. Cold patch kits are best for emergency repairs on the road.

Hot Patch Repair

1. Remove the tube from tire as described under *Tire Removal* in this chapter.

2. Roughen area around hole slightly larger than the patch (**Figure 32**). Use a pocket knife or similar tool to scrape the tube; be careful that you don't cause further damage.

3. Remove the backing from patch.

CAUTION
Do not touch newly exposed rubber with your fingers. This will prevent a good seal.

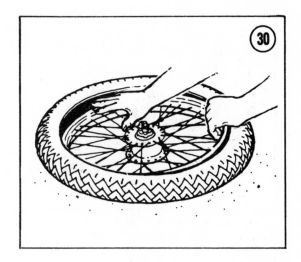

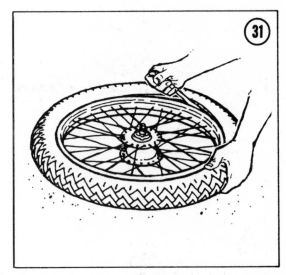

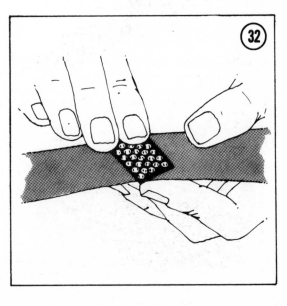

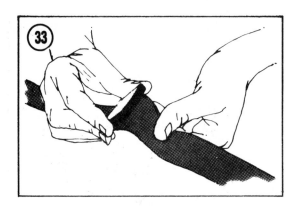

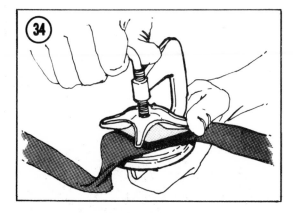

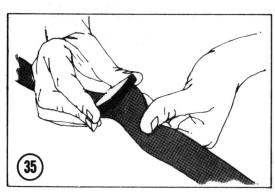

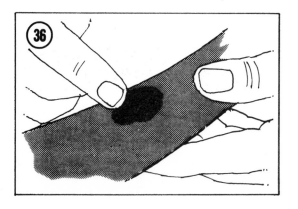

4. Center the patch over hole (**Figure 33**).

5. Install clamp around tube so that it holds the fuel container over the patch (**Figure 34**).

6. Pry up a corner of the fuel and light it. Let all of the fuel burn away.

CAUTION
The clamp gets hot, so don't touch it until it cools.

7. Remove the clamp and peel the tube off the fuel container (**Figure 35**).

Cold Patch Repair

1. Remove the tube from tire as described under *Tire Removal* in this chapter.

2. Roughen area around hole slightly larger than the patch; use a cap from tire repair kit or pocket knife. Do not scrape too vigorously or you may cause additional damage.

3. Apply a small quantity of special cement to the puncture and spread it evenly with a finger (**Figure 36**).

4. Allow cement to dry until tacky — usually 30 seconds or so is sufficient.

5. Remove the backing from the patch.

CAUTION
Do not touch the newly exposed rubber with your fingers or the patch will not stick firmly.

6. Center patch over hole. Hold patch firmly in place for about 30 seconds to allow the cement to set (**Figure 37**).

7. Dust the patched area with talcum powder to prevent sticking.

7

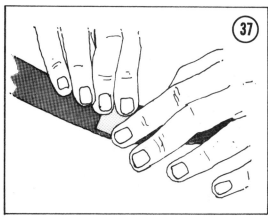

CHAPTER EIGHT

STEERING, SUSPENSION, AND FRAME

This chapter includes repair and replacement procedures for steering, front forks, swing arm and frame components.

HANDLEBARS

Removal/Installation

1. Disconnect the front brake and clutch cable from the hand levers.
2. Remove the ignition switch.
3. Remove the 2 screws (**Figure 1**) securing the throttle housing and remove it.
4. Remove the 4 bolts securing the handlebar holders (**Figure 2**) and remove them and the handlebars.
5. Install by reversing the removal steps. Tighten the bolts securing the handlebars to 6-9 ft.-lb. (8-12 N•m).

Inspection

Check the handlebars for bending or other damage. Check the brake and clutch cables for chafing or damage. Replace if necessary.

STEERING HEAD

Refer to **Figure 3** for this procedure.

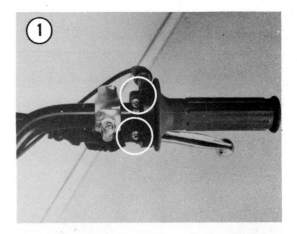

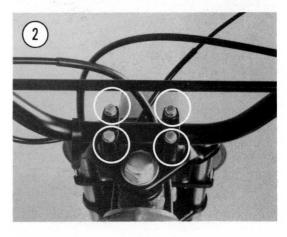

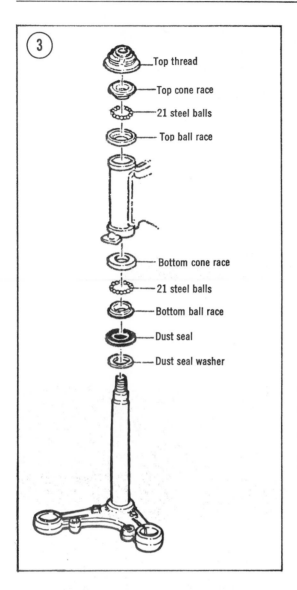

- Top thread
- Top cone race
- 21 steel balls
- Top ball race
- Bottom cone race
- 21 steel balls
- Bottom ball race
- Dust seal
- Dust seal washer

Disassembly

1. Remove the front wheel as described under *Front Wheel Removal/Installation* in Chapter Seven.

2. Remove the handlebars as described under *Handlebars Removal/Installation* in this chapter.

3. Unscrew the steering stem nut (A, **Figure 4**).

4. Remove the right and left fork top bolts (B, **Figure 4**) and remove the top fork bridge.

5. Loosen the lower fork bridge bolts (**Figure 5**).

6. Slide the entire fork assembly and fender assembly out.

7. Remove the adjuster nut with a pin spanner or use an easily improvised unit as shown in **Figure 6**.

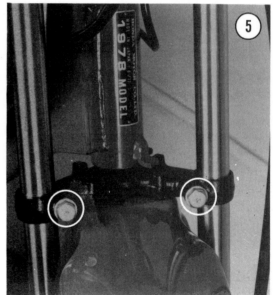

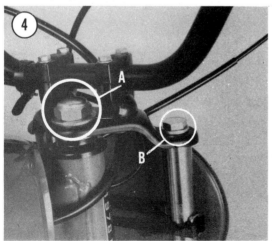

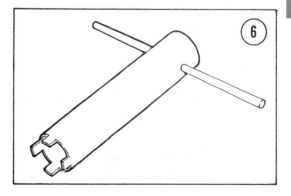

8

8. Have an assistant hold a large pan under the steering stem to catch the loose ball bearings and carefully lower the steering stem (**Figure 7**).

> NOTE: *There are 42 balls total — 21 on both the top and bottom.*

Inspection

1. Clean the bearing races in the steering head, the steering stem races and all the ball bearings with solvent.

2. Check for broken welds on the frame around the steering head.

3. Check each of the balls for pitting, scratches or discoloration indicating wear or corrosion. *Replace them in sets if any are bad.*

4. Check upper and lower races in the steering head. See *Bearing Race Replacement* if races are pitted, scratched, or badly worn.

5. Check steering stem for cracks. Check bearing race on stem for pitting, scratches, or excessive wear.

6. Check inside of steering head adjuster (top ball race) for pitting, scratches, or excessive wear.

Bearing Race Replacement

The headset and steering stem bearing races are pressed into place. Because they are easily bent, do not remove them unless they are worn and require replacement. Take old races to the dealer to ensure exact replacement.

To remove a headset race, insert a hardwood stick into the head tube and carefully tap the race out from the inside (**Figure 8**). Tap all around the race so that neither the race nor the head tube are bent. To install a race, fit it into the end of the head tube. Tap it slowly and squarely with a block of wood (**Figure 9**).

> NOTE: *The upper and lower races are different. Be sure that you install them at the proper ends of the head tube.*

Steering Stem Race and Dust Seal Removal/Installation

To remove the steering stem race, try twisting and pulling it up by hand. If it will not come off, carefully pry it up with a screwdriver, while working around in a circle, prying a little at a time. Remove the dust seal and the washer.

Install the washer and new dust seal. Slide the race over the steering stem with the bearing surface pointing up. Tap the race down with a piece of hardwood, work around in a circle so that the race will not be bent. Make sure it is seated squarely and all the way down.

Assembly

Refer to **Figure 3** for this procedure.

1. Make sure the steering head and stem races are properly seated.

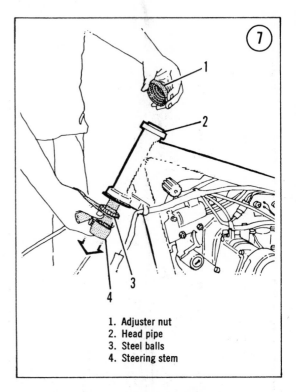

1. Adjuster nut
2. Head pipe
3. Steel balls
4. Steering stem

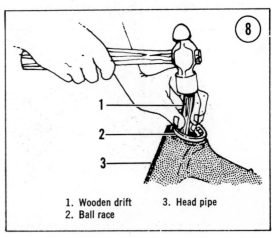

1. Wooden drift
2. Ball race
3. Head pipe

2. Install bottom bearing race cone over steering stem. Slide it down as far as possible.

3. Apply a coat of grease to bottom race cone and fit 21 ball bearings around it (**Figure 10**). The grease will hold them in place.

4. Fit 21 ball bearings into top race (**Figure 11**) in head tube. Grease will hold them in place.

5. Insert steering stem into head tube. Hold it firmly in place.

6. Install top bearing race cone.

7. Screw steering stem adjuster nut onto stem.

8. Tighten adjuster firmly to seat bearings. Use the pin spanner or tool shown in **Figure 6**.

9. Loosen adjuster until there is noticeable play in stem.

10. Tighten adjuster until there is just enough to remove all play, both horizontal and vertical (**Figure 12**), yet loose enough so that the assembly will turn to the locks under its own weight after an initial assist.

11. Install the top fork bridge.

12. Install the fork and fender assembly.

13. Install the top fork bridge and bolts.

14. Tighten the lower fork bridge bolts to 14-22 ft.-lb. (19-30 N•m).

15. Install the steering stem nut and tighten to 43-65 ft.-lb. (58-88 N•m).

16. Install the handlebars and front wheel as described in this chapter.

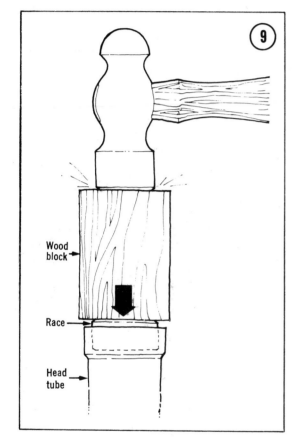

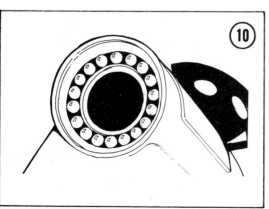

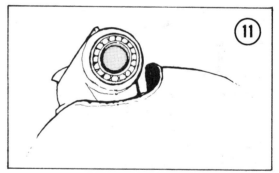

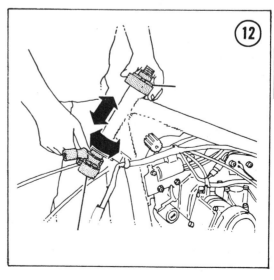

8

Steering Stem Adjustment

If play develops in the steering system, it may only require adjustment. However, don't take a chance on it. Disassemble the stem and look for possible damage. Then reassemble and adjust as described in Steps 9-11, *Steering Head Assembly* in this chapter.

FRONT FORKS

The Honda front suspension consists of a spring-controlled, hydraulically dampened telescopic fork. Before suspecting major trouble, drain the fork oil and refill with the proper type and quantity; refer to Chapter Four. If you still have trouble, such as poor dampening, tendency to bottom out or top out, or leakage around the rubber seals, then follow the service procedures in this section.

To simplify fork service and to prevent the mixing of parts, the legs should be removed, serviced and reinstalled individually.

Removal/Installation

1. Remove the front wheel as described under *Front Wheel Removal/Installation* in Chapter Seven.

2. Remove the bolts securing the front fender and remove it.

3. Loosen the lower fork bridge bolt (**Figure 13**).

4. Remove the upper fork bolt (**Figure 14**).

5. Remove the fork tube out through the bottom. It may be necessary to slightly rotate the tube while removing it.

> NOTE: *There may be rust in the area of the lower fork bridge and the tube. Apply some WD-40 onto the area prior to removal. Also insert a screwdriver into the slit on the lower fork bridge to help in the removal.*

6. Install by reversing the removal steps. Tighten the lower fork bridge bolts to 14-22 ft.-lb. (19-30 N•m). Tighten the axle nut to 29-40 ft.-lb. (39-54 N•m) and install a *new* cotter pin.

Disassembly

Refer to **Figure 15** for this procedure.

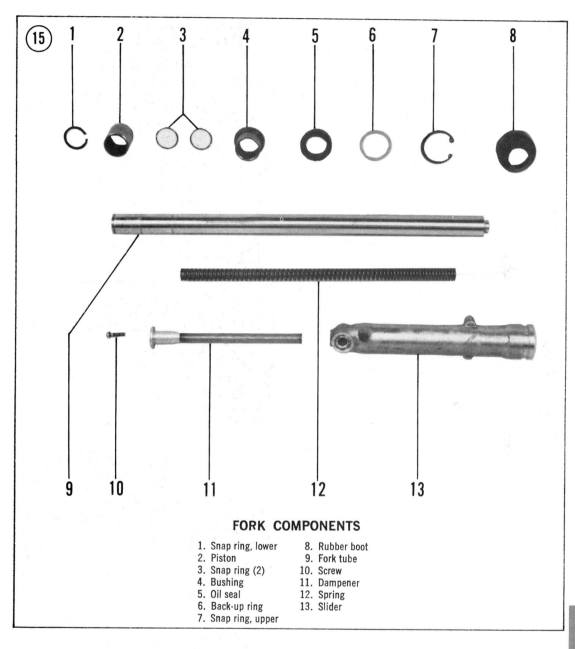

FORK COMPONENTS

1. Snap ring, lower	8. Rubber boot
2. Piston	9. Fork tube
3. Snap ring (2)	10. Screw
4. Bushing	11. Dampener
5. Oil seal	12. Spring
6. Back-up ring	13. Slider
7. Snap ring, upper	

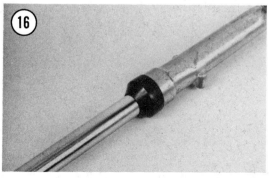

1. Remove the rubber boot (**Figure 16**) out of the notch in the slider and slide it off of the fork tube.

2. Remove the snap ring (**Figure 17**) with snap ring pliers.

3. Remove the back-up ring.

4. Pull the slider out of the fork tube. Some resistance will be felt as the seal is a snug fit.

5. Empty the fork oil. *Do not reuse it*.

6. Remove the spring.

8

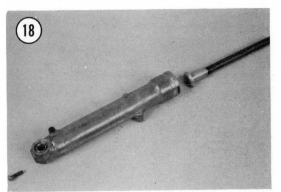

7. Remove the screw **(Figure 18)** securing the dampener into the slide and remove it.

8. Remove the snap ring **(Figure 19)** on the bottom of the fork tube and remove the piston, piston stop rings (2), bushing, and oil seal.

Inspection

1. Thoroughly clean all parts in solvent and dry. Check the fork tubes for signs of wear or galling.

2. Check the dampener rod for straightness. **Figure 20** shows one method. The rod should be replaced if the runout is 0.008 in. (0.2mm) or greater.

3. Inspect the oil seal for scoring or nicks and for loss of resiliency. Replace if its condition is questionable.

4. Measure the outside diameter of the piston. If its diameter is 1.2165 in. (30.90mm) or smaller it must be replaced.

5. Measure the inside diameter of the lower fork slider **(Figure 21)**. If its dimension is 1.2276 in. (31.18mm) or greater it must be replaced.

6. Any parts that are worn or damaged should be replaced; simply cleaning and reinstalling unserviceable components will not improve performance of the front suspension.

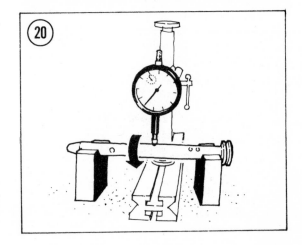

Assembly

1. Slide the oil seal onto the fork tube from the lower end of the tube only **(Figure 22)**.

CAUTION
The lower end of the fork tube has a chamfer on it and will not damage the seal; the upper end will cause damage to the seal.

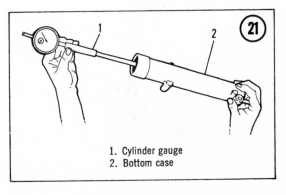

1. Cylinder gauge
2. Bottom case

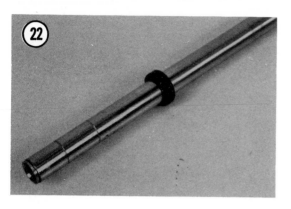

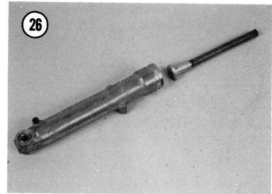

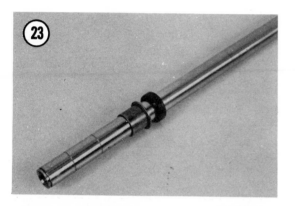

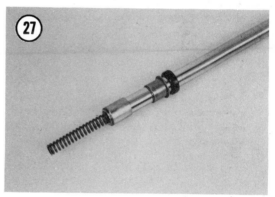

2. Install the bushing (**Figure 23**).

3. Install the 2 snap rings (**Figure 24**).

4. Install the piston (**Figure 25**) with the recess toward the snap ring.

5. Install the lower snap ring.

6. Install the dampener rod into the slider and secure it with the screw (**Figure 26**).

7. Insert the spring into the fork tube (**Figure 27**).

> NOTE: *Install the end with the coils the closest together into the tube.*

8. Install the fork tube into the slider.

9. Insert the rubber oil seal into the slider. The seal must be tapped or pressed into place. Use a piece of pipe (**Figure 28**) with an inside diameter of 1¼ in. (31.75mm) and an outside diameter of 1½ in. (38.1mm). Place the piece of pipe in a vise and tap on the slider until the oil seal is seated. Be sure that the back-up ring is in place.

10. Install the snap ring; again make sure the back-up ring is in position between the oil seal and the snap ring (**Figure 17**).

8

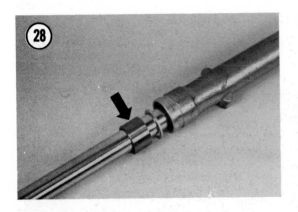

11. Install the rubber boot.

12. Fill the fork tube with 3.7 oz. (110cc) of fresh automatic transmission fluid or fork oil **(Figure 29)**.

> NOTE: *To measure the correct amount of fluid, use a plastic baby bottle. These have measured increments in fluid ounces (oz.) and cubic centimeters (cc) on the side (**Figure 30**). Many fork oil containers have a semi-transparent strip on the side of the bottle (**Figure 31**) to aid in the measuring.*

REAR SHOCKS

The rear shocks are spring controlled and hydraulically dampened. Spring preload can be adjusted by rotating the cam ring at the base of the spring **(Figure 32)** — *clockwise to increase* preload and *counterclockwise to decrease* it. Both cams must be indexed on the same detent. The shocks are sealed and cannot be rebuilt. Service is limited to removal and replacement of the hydraulic unit.

Removal/Installation

Removal and installation of the rear shocks is easier if they are done separately. The remaining unit will support the rear of the bike and maintain the correct relationship between the top and bottom mounts.

1. Block up the engine or support the bike in a true vertical position.

2. Adjust both shocks to their softest setting, *completely counterclockwise.*

3. Remove the upper and lower acorn nuts **(Figure 33)**.

8

4. Pull the shock off.

5. Install by reversing removal steps. Torque the shock nuts to 22-29 ft.-lb. (30-39 N•m).

SWING ARM

Under normal use the swing arm bushings have a long service life. However, in time the bushings will wear and must be replaced. Indications of excessive bushing wear are imprecise steering and a tendency for the motorcycle to pull to one side or the other during acceleration and braking.

Removal/Installation

1. Remove the exhaust system as described under *Exhaust System Removal/Installation* in Chapter Six.

2. Block up the bike to remove the weight from the rear wheel.

3. Remove the rear wheel as described under *Rear Wheel Removal/Installation* in Chapter Seven.

4. Remove the acorn nuts (**Figure 33**) on the lower end of the shock.

NOTE: *It is not necessary to completely remove the shocks.*

5. Withdraw the swing arm pivot bolt from the left-hand side (**Figure 34**).

6. Pull the swing arm, complete with chain guard and rear brake torque arm, down and out to the rear to remove.

7. Install by reversing the removal steps. Tighten the swing arm pivot bolt nut to 22-29 ft.-lb. (30-39 N•m).

Inspection

Thoroughly clean and dry all parts. Slide the pivot bolt back into the swing arm and check for radial play. If any play can be felt, the bushings, and possibly the pivot bolt, should be replaced.

Replace any parts that are questionable. If only one of the bushings is bad, it is best to replace both of them.

KICKSTAND (SIDE STAND)

Removal/Installation

1. Block up the engine.

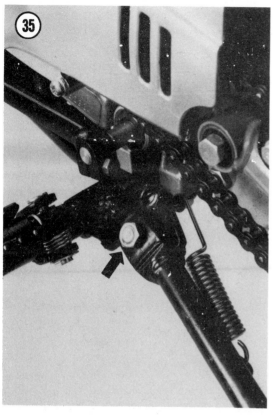

2. Raise the kickstand so the spring is in the relaxed position.

3. Disconnect the spring from the frame with Vise Grips.

4. Unbolt the kickstand from the frame (**Figure 35**).

5. Install by reversing the removal steps. Apply a light coat of multipurpose grease to the pivot surfaces of the frame and kickstand prior to installation.

FOOTPEGS

Replacement

Remove the 4 bolts (**Figure 36**) securing the footpeg assembly and engine scuff plate to the engine and remove it. Install by installing the 4 bolts.

FRAME

The frame does not require periodic maintenance. However, all welds should be examined immediately after any accident, even a slight one.

8

Component Removal/Installation

1. Remove the fuel tank and seat.

2. Remove the engine as described in Chapter Five.

3. Remove the front wheel, steering, and suspension components as described in Chapters Seven and Eight.

4. Remove the rear wheel and suspension components. See Chapters Seven and Eight.

5. Remove the wiring harness and ignition coil.

6. Remove the kickstand as described in this chapter.

7. Remove the bearing races from the steering head tube as described in this chapter.

8. Check the frame for bends, cracks, or other damage, especially around welded joints and areas which are rusted.

9. Assemble by reversing the removal steps.

Stripping and Painting

Remove all components from the frame. Thoroughly strip off all old paint. The best way is to have it sandblasted down to bare metal. If this is not possible, you can use a liquid paint remover like Strypeeze, or equivalent, and steel wool and a fine hard wire brush.

When the frame is down to bare metal, have it inspected for hairline and internal cracks. Magnafluxing is the most common process.

Make sure that the primer is compatible with the type of paint you are going to use for the final coat. Spray one or two coats of primer as smoothly as possible. Let it dry thoroughly and use a fine grade of wet sandpaper (400-600 grit) to remove any flaws. Carefully wipe clean the surface and then spray the final coat. Use either lacquer or enamel and follow the manufacturer's instructions.

A shop specializing in painting will probably do the best job. However, you can do a surprisingly good job with a good grade of spray paint. Spend a few extra bucks and get a good grade of paint as it will make a difference in how well it looks and how long it will stand up. One trick in using spray paints is to first shake the can thoroughly — make sure the ball inside the can is loose, if not return it and get a good one. Shake the can as long as is stated on the can. Then immerse the can *upright* in a pot or bucket of *warm water (not hot — not over 120°F)*.

> **WARNING**
> *Higher temperatures could cause the can to burst.* **Do not** *place the can in direct contact with any flame or heat source.*

Leave the can in for several minutes. When thoroughly warmed, shake the can again and spray the frame. Several light mist coats are better than one heavy coat. Spray painting is best done in temperatures of 70°-80°F, any temperature above or below this will give you problems.

After the final coat has dried completely, at least 48 hours, any overspray or orange peel may be removed with *a light application* of rubbing compound and finished with polishing compound. Be careful not to rub too hard and go through the finish.

Finish off with a couple of good coats of wax prior to reassembling all the components.

Table 1   FRAME SPECIFICATIONS

	1975-76	1977-78
Frame type	Single down tube, stamped backbone	Single down tube, stamped backbone
Front fork travel	4.1 in. (104mm)	4.9 in. (126mm)
Rear fork travel	2.4 in. (62mm)	3.3 in. (84.6mm)
Front tire size	2.50 x 16	2.50 x 16
Front tire pressure	17 psi (1.2kg/cm²)	17 psi (1.2kg/cm²)
Rear tire size	3.00 x 14	3.00 x 14
Rear tire pressure	20 psi (1.4kg/cm²)	20 psi (1.4kg/cm²)
Fuel capacity	1.2 gal. (4.5 liter)	0.8 gal. (3.0 liter)
Caster angle	28 degrees	27.5 degrees
Trail	3.3 in. (82mm)	3.0 in. (78mm)
Brake drum I.D. (front and rear)	4.3228-4.3386 in. (109.8-110.2mm)	4.3228-4.3386 in. (109.8-110.2mm)
Shoe thickness (front and rear)	0.1535-0.1614 in. (3.9-4.1mm)	0.1535-0.1614 in. (3.9-4.1mm)
Rear spring free length	7.4291 in. (188.7mm)	7.4291 in. (188.7mm)

Table 2   FRAME TORQUE VALUES

Item	Ft.-lb.	N•m
Steering stem nut	43-65	58-88
Handlebar holder	6-9	8-12
Front fork lower bridge bolts	14-22	19-30
Front axle nut	29-40	39-54
Rear axle nut	29-40	39-54
Rear brake torque arm	7-14	9-19
Rear fork pivot bolt	22-29	30-39
Rear shock absorber	22-29	30-39
Rear brake arm	6-9	8-12
Foot peg assembly	14-22	19-30
Engine mounting bolts	14-22	19-30
Engine mounting plate bolts	11-18	15-24
Shift lever and kickstarter lever	6-9	8-12
Spokes	1-1.5	1.5-2.0

8

CHAPTER NINE

PERFORMANCE IMPROVEMENT

Honda's XR75 was a revolutionary step forward in minibikes — for the first time a small two-wheeler was available that was designed to look, handle, and function as a true motorcycle instead of a recreational compromise.

Most testers and evaluators assessed the XR as an extraordinary machine — a bike which would be ideal for smaller people around camps and in parks as a recreational toy, with its absolutely indestructible and non-temperamental engine, ease of maintenance and reliability. In short, it was an outstanding playbike.

But thousands of kids knew better — they saw the XR75 as their entry into serious racing. And, in a few short months, they proved they were right. The XR75 became the top-rated winner in the tough minicycle competition arena.

With the XR's successes in racing, an entire subindustry got started, building high performance accessories for the XR75, from simple bolt-on shocks and fork boots to sophisticated and expensive monoshock custom frames.

An essential part of high performance is that the more money you spend, the faster you can go. This is certainly true with the XR75. It is possible to spend well over $2,000 building a completely customized racer, using nothing more than off-the-shelf performance parts.

However, before an owner/rider gets into very deep financial water spending this kind of money he should consider two facts:

1. In one or two years, he will be too large to ride the XR75 competitively. At that time, the only option will be to sell the XR and move up to a fullsize motorcycle.

2. Resale value, like the initial cost, of the XR75 is quite low. This is especially true for competition-modified bikes. You would be very lucky sell that $2500 supertrick XR75 for much over $500 — a very serious loss. In addition, bikes which have been raced are usually hard to sell. They may be too exotic for what the prospective owner wants. Also, a sensible buyer realizes that competition machinery has almost certainly been raced hard which means flogged, sometimes to the point of breakage.

Another area of consideration for the potential XR75 high performance builder/rider to consider is the competitiveness of today's super-sophisticated minicyle racing scene.

Two years ago, the XR was easily able to destroy its competitors, those minicycles still designed as utility toys. But with the XR's success, other manufacurers have gotten into the market. And while the XR75 essentially hasn't seen that many changes since its introduction, the new bikes from other makers are as finely designed in their up-to-the minute engineering as any currently available fullsize motocross machine.

A stock XR75 can be beaten easily by either Suzuki's RM or Yamaha's YZ. When given a full modification package, of course, the Honda can walk away from either of the two bikes.

Unfortunately, when so modified, it can't run in stock classes any more, but must graduate to modified racing. And, in the modified classes, the built-up XR will run against equally hotrodded YZ's and RM's. Against competition like that, the XR75 cannot be made competitive. National minicycle racing has proven this over the past year or so, as the XR75 has slowly disappeared from the winner's circle.

The rider who is willing to spend the money for a vastly-modified machine will also be very serious about wanting to win. So the racer-to-be would be better off starting with one of the faster or better-handling Yamahas or Suzukis. has a number of advantages. First, the XR75 is a four-stroke, so it can be easily silenced to an acceptable noise output level while still retaining impressive performance characteristics — a drawback for most two-strokes.

Second, with some improvements to the performance, the XR75 is an excellent bike to learn riding style and techniques on — a machine which retains tractability, is easy to ride and quite forgiving. A totally-modified performance machine such as the YZ will require long hours of maintenance and a high degree of skill to ride properly. A winning two-stroke will also have a very narrow powerband. Only a skilled and experienced rider will be able to keep the rpm's where they must be and therefore become a winner.

Last and most importantly is the XR75's reliability. Very few people would rather work on their bikes than ride them. And the XR, either in stock or in significantly modified form will retain its bulletproof qualities.

THE MOST FROM STOCK

Too many riders spend time leafing through the catalogs, dreaming about the high performance parts they'll put on their XR to turn it into a rocketship. Meanwhile, their bike sits in the garage with plugs which have not been looked at in six months, oil which has the consistency of black cottage cheese, points that are set to a plus or minus figure of half an inch, and valves which are so loose they sound like a tin can factory.

The beginning of high performance is a correctly tuned and maintained bike. Learn to do the work yourself using this book's tune-up chapter. It'll give you experience and familiarity with your machine, and it won't be a somewhat mysterious collection of nuts and bolts. Also, as you become more skilled in maintenance, you'll find yourself doing a better and more careful job than any dealer or paid-by-the-hour mechanic. People take better care of their own property than they do other people's property.

PLANNING PERFORMANCE

Most motorcycle owners find themselves modifying their bikes bit by bit, as they can afford it and as their riding skills improve.

This is an excellent policy, since it keeps the rider from overbuilding his machine, and ending up with a bike which is peaky, unreliable, and frightening to ride. And a racer will go far faster on a machine that he isn't a little afraid of.

If a performance program is laid out step-by-step (this month is the month for a performance pipe, next month buy a cam, the third month is for a big bore kit), each step will be made at the correct time. There is no point in paying for a porting job, for example, until the engine modifications are almost complete. Otherwise, when you add a big bore kit, or different cam, the headwork won't be correct for the new engine.

One way to conserve money when involved in a building program is to add high-performance parts when the stock parts wear out. Frequently, the performance part you want will be less expensive than the OEM part from your dealer. For example, when the standard air filter is clogged beyond cleaning or use, it can be replaced with a Uni sock-type filter, even though you haven't gotten to carburetor modifications on your program yet.

9

Performance modifications will be outlined in this chapter on a step-by-step basis, beginning with suspension modifications. Most riders find that the stock engine can exceed the limitations of the stock suspension. The first step toward winning is to make the machine handle better.

SUSPENSION

The first changes to the XR's suspension will be very noticeable and will make large improvements in the handling. However, as the rider continues adding to his XR, those changes may be harder and harder to be aware of, and the improvements will become smaller and smaller.

Realizing the two areas of caution on the XR75 (money invested that you won't realize on resale, plus very expensive changes which still won't make the bike competitive in the modified classes), a good tool to work with in suspension modifications is your own test course.

Ideally, it should be something like a large and fairly rough vacant lot, a ways from where you'll bother people. Lay out a mini-course, with a few normal whoop-de-doos, a washboard section, a jump and so forth.

Ride the course — it needn't be very long — until you're very familiar with it. Then get a friend with an inexpensive stopwatch to time you on five of six laps. Use those times to get a lap average. Only use those times which are very close to each other — if you bobble a lap, don't use that time.

With your own test course, you can now do two things:

1. As you make each change to the suspension system, you can see how much of an improvement has been made. When you start hitting flat times — a change or two doesn't affect your lap time — then you've hit the limits either of the bike or of your current riding ability. Also, if you make changes and your times keep dropping right up to the point where you're ready for a very expensive custom frame, you know it's time to move up to the RM or YZ racers, or else to a fullsize motorcycle.

2. With competition suspension components, quite a bit of tuning is possible, such as making

sure that the spring weight on the shocks is correct, or if you're using aircaps on your forks, what the correct air preload is. With your testing course, you can make an adjustment, run a few laps and get times, and be able to tell whether that adjustment is actually improving the suspension.

The adjustments you make on your own course won't necessarily be valid for all riding conditions. For example, on a track which is smoother than you mini-course, you could very well use a lighter spring than normal. On a rougher course, the reverse would apply.

Shocks

The stock rear shocks used on the XR75 are marginal for use in low speed fireroading. For competition purposes, they should be replaced.

Picking shocks is a little like picking your own favorite oil among the top brands. A lot of riders have preferences, and those preferences are obviously founded on what works *for them* or, in the case of some sponsored riders, what they're paid to use.

Cost should be a consideration when picking shocks for your XR — it's possible to spend well over $200 for the super-competition brands of gas shocks, such as Foxx. But for most competition riders, a set of these extremely sophisticated shocks isn't needed — they won't be able to ride up to that extreme point where these suspension components make the difference.

Two relatively inexpensive shocks which come well-recommended by racers are from S&W (**Figure 1**) and Number One Products (**Figure 2**). They're available in 11-inch lengths for the early (pre-1977) models and 12-inch lengths for the later XR's.

Either model will offer very precise damping, have a number of variable rate springs available, and have an extraordinarily long lifespan which should be sufficient for the riding life of the XR75.

More expensive, but offering greater advantages particularly on rougher courses, are the Number One remote reservoir gas shocks. With the small reservoir mounted to the side of each shock, a greater volume of damping material is available. In addition, with the reservoir, the

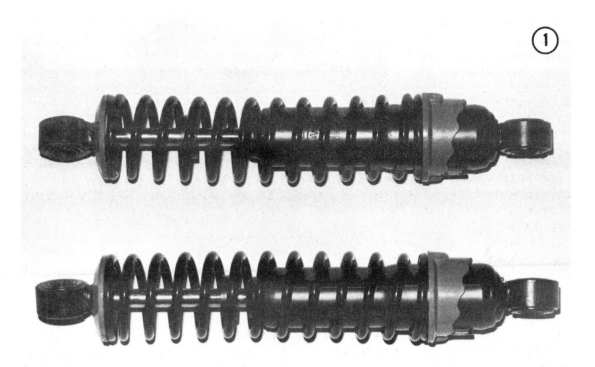

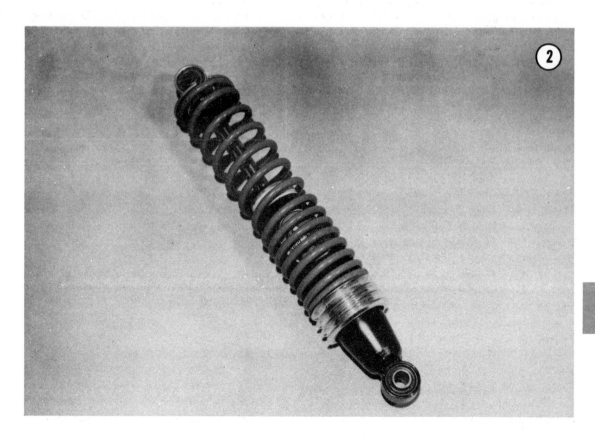

9

damping fluid cannot overheat and become ineffective.

Once a pair of shocks are selected, springs must be chosen carefully. Generally, on the XR75, a single-rate spring of between 30 and 70 pounds should be chosen. A beginning point for the average size rider on normal tracks should be 55 pounds if the shocks are still conventionally mounted.

Forward-Mounted Shock Kits

The paramount concern on any offroad bike is that the suspension keeps the rear wheel on the ground as much as possible. Only when power is going to the ground can speed and throttle-controlled directional changes be made. Obviously, the larger the amount of rear wheel travel, the more likely the wheel is to stay down.

With shocks in their standard mounting position, there is a limited amount of rear wheel travel possible — it can only move until the shock absorbers bottom or top out.

Several ways exist to increase this travel, such as increased shock length, relocating the shocks to a vertical midpoint mounting on the swing arm, and forward-mounting the shocks in what is commonly called a "laydown" position.

Of all of these modifications, the least expensive is with a weld-on forward shock position kit. New tabs, to mount the top of the shock, are heliarced to the frame forward of the stock mounting holes. This kit, available from PK Racing, will generally increase the available rear wheel travel by an inch or two.

Some experimentation may have to be made with heavier springs once the conversion is complete, since, with increased leverage the springs will, in effect, be lighter than before. However, it is recommended that considerable riding be done before springs are changed, since many riders find, in practical experience, that the same poundage of springs is the most satisfactory.

Front Forks

Unlike the rear shocks, the stock front forks on the XR75 offer fairly decent performance.

Fork travel may be improved by installing a set of S&W fork springs. This will stiffen up the forks, and give another ½ inch of travel.

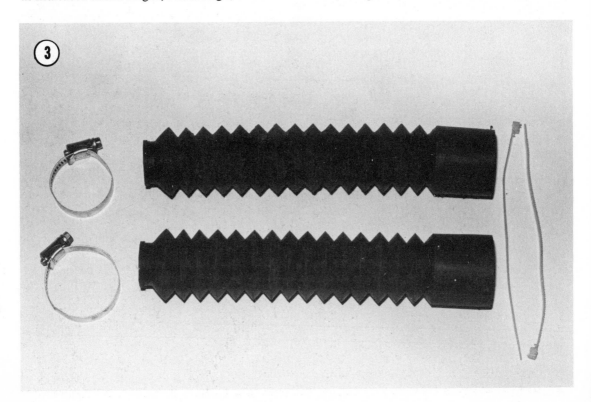

Bel-Ray SAE10 fork oil should be used in the front forks in place of the specified stock fluid.

PK Racing sells a set of airfork caps for the XR75. These caps replace the stock fork caps, and are fitted with air fittings. Air pressure may be added to the forks to preload them. In theory, this preloading would somewhat improve fork performance, particularly with a heavy rider.

However, most riders who have experimented with these aircaps have found little benefit gained. A slight drawback is that, with increased air pressure internally, the fork seals may have a slightly shortened lifespan.

Seal life may be improved by installing PK fork boots **(Figure 3)**. These are not only colorful, but will keep dirt out of the forks far better than the stock boots.

Stock damping on the forks may be considered quite good. However, very competitive riders or those racing on very rough tracks may replace the stock damping assembly with a kit from Number One Products **(Figure 4)**. Damping will be improved, but with significantly increased wear. The forks will need to be disassembled regularly, and the hard rider can expect the rods to need occasional replacement.

Fanatics who are concerned about removing the ultimate amount of unsprung weight from the forks may have the lower fork legs turned down on a lathe slightly. This should *only* be done by an experienced motorcycle performance shop, as it is very easy to structurally weaken the fork legs with this modification. In any event, this turning-down will only reduce the weight of the legs by about ½ pound. For this reason, it's not worth the considerable expense for most riders.

Heavier riders, or those on rugged courses, may experience some problem with the forks tweaking slightly.

Installation of a Circle Industries aluminum fork brace **(Figure 5)** will reduce this.

In really extreme cases (assuming the stock parts are in good condition and there are no loose parts), it may be necessary to replace the stock triple clamp mechanism with custom-made aluminum parts from Pro Fab.

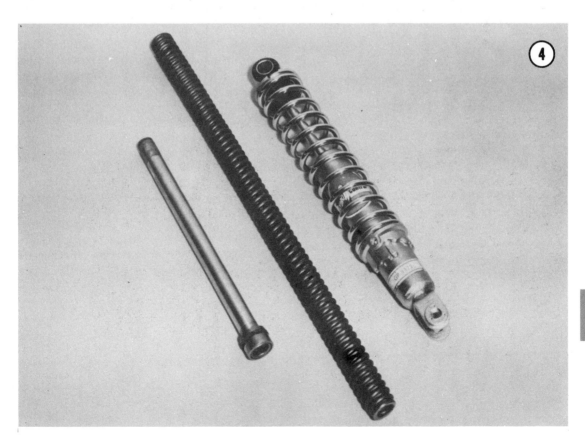

Swing Arm

Some swing arm side play may occur under severe handling stresses. The simplest solution is to replace the stock swing arm with a boxed accessory part from Pro Tec. In addition to being far stronger than stock, the new swing arm will give the option of a superior lower shock mounting position.

Frames

The last stage in suspension modification is to junk the existing frame and replace it with a custom-made Pro Tec frame. This is an extremely expensive modification (over $300 for the bare frame) and, as mentioned previously, it still will not guarantee the XR75 a place in the winner's circle.

Pro Tec offers two different frame models. Both are heliarc welded 4130 chrome moly tubing, and considerably lighter and stronger than the stock component.

The lower priced frame is set up for a laydown style shock mounting position, with the shock angle canted far forward. Rear wheel travel will be markedly improved with this frame.

The higher-priced frame converts the XR into a monoshock bike like the currently-competitive motocross machines (**Figure 6**). A 13.5 inch Girling shock mounts under the top frame tube, and is connected via a Y-brace to the rear axle. Set up, the monoshock XR (**Figure 7**) will have a full seven inches of rear wheel travel.

The advantage of a monoshock frame is that, with a huge amount of rear wheel travel, the wheel will stay on the ground under most riding conditions.

There are two major disadvantages to a monoshock frame. First, the bike will be very tall in the saddle, due to the extended amount of rear wheel travel. It may be too tall for short-legged riders to sit on comfortably.

The second problem is more severe. With the monoshock frame, the fork and steering head angle will be subject to constant variation. This means that the bike itself will have a considerable variation in its handling characteristics, depending on how far the monoshock is compressed. For highly skilled riders, this problem may be lived with for the advantage of

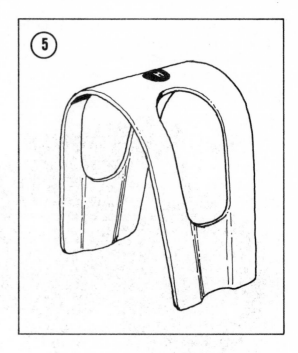

the traction. However, for many riders the constant change may actually lessen their lap times, particularly on smoother terrain.

The final drawback to the Pro Tec monoshock frame is its order time — since the XR has ceased to be truly competitive, the demand for super-exotic competition parts has become less and less. Pro Tec will still custom build the monoshock, but only after five or more orders have been received. This means that the wait after the order has been put in could be considerable.

Neither of these frames can be considered a recommended modification, due to their expense and the inherent lack of competitiveness of the XR75.

Wheels

Handling will be improved by replacing the stock front wheel with a 17-inch alloy wheel from PK Racing. The larger wheel is not only lighter, but the size will increase gyroscopic action — thereby improving the wheel/fork assembly's ability to maintain a given tracking direction.

Tires

There are a wide assortment of tires available for use on the XR75. One of the best is made by

Cheng Shin, which should be used as a replacement when the 17-inch front wheel is installed.

On the rear, a heavy rider or a rider on fairly smooth tracks should keep the stock tire size. A lighter rider might change to a 3.60 x 14 section.

Under no circumstances should a super-wide tire be used. While this will increase the size of the tire print on the ground, it will also reduce the loading of the contact patch. Consequently, it will take less of a bump or shock for the tire to leave the ground, which will mean lessened traction and control. Which, ultimately, means loss of speed, precision, and possibly, the race.

ENGINE

The XR75 engine is capable of rather awesome development. In stock form, it develops perhaps $4\frac{1}{2}$ horsepower. A completely built and modified competition engine, in a high state of tune, may put out as much as $13\frac{1}{2}$ horsepower at peak rpm. And it will do it with an acceptable degree of reliability. Of course, such an engine should not be built if the bike is to be used for anything other than racing — a mill in such a high state of tune will no longer be suitable for casual cow trailing or riding round campsites. Owners wishing to retain some degree of general usage for their XR75's would be best advised to make more moderate performance improvements.

As with the suspension, building up the engine should be done step-by-step, both to avoid dealing a deathblow to your budget and also to make sure you're only building what you need and want to ride.

Exhaust

One of the most critical factors these days in the design of OEM exhaust systems is the currently allowable noise standards. Obviously, as the maximum permissable noise level decreases, a bike's exhaust must be more and more restrictive and hence power-robbing.

It is a tribute to the design genius of Honda engineers that they have managed to equip the XR75 with an exhaust system which still permits the engine to develop a great deal of power without producing an ear-splitting exhaust noise level.

For performance purposes, the beginning point is to replace the stock exhaust system with a high performance pipe.

However, this should be done cautiously if the bike will be ridden on anything other than a competition course.

Noise pollution from motorcycles has been responsible for most of the land closure regulations over the past few years.

While you, the rider/builder of a bike, may delight in the sound of your built-up XR's engine screaming through a wide-open exhaust, the other users of public land most definitely do not.

It is not a matter of who's right or wrong, nor of what you may wish to do. The point is that rights, particularly in the use of the wild areas, must only go so far as to not interfere with others' enjoyment of those areas.

NOTE: *Use of open, gutted, or exceptionally noisy exhausts is totally unforgiveable. Not only will there be no added power developed from just an open pipe, but horsepower will actually be decreased. In addition, actual engine damage may result from such a practice. More importantly, riders who run open exhausts are a black mark for all motorcyclists. Their actions may result not only in the closing of their own favorite riding areas, but anti-motorcycle opinions being formed by non-riders, which will encourage the passage of even more anti-motorcycle legislation.*

Even with the use of a relatively quiet high performance exhaust system, the rider should always make sure a spark arrester is installed on the bike before it is ridden in any non-racetrack offroad area. This is a legal necessity on all public lands and a moral necessity on *all* lands. A Bassani spark arrester (**Figure 8**) may be easily clamped on almost all available performance exhaust systems for the XR75.

Picking the correct exhaust system is difficult, particularly when there are so many models available for the XR. However, among those which have been successful on the racetrack are those from PK Racing (**Figure 9**) and Bassani. Bassani, in fact, offers three models of pipe for the early XR75 and two for the later XR75. These are, for the 1973-1976

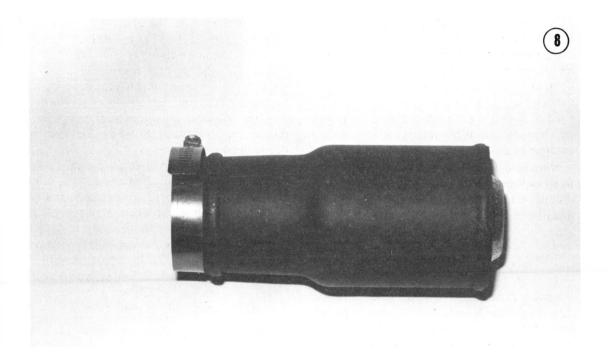

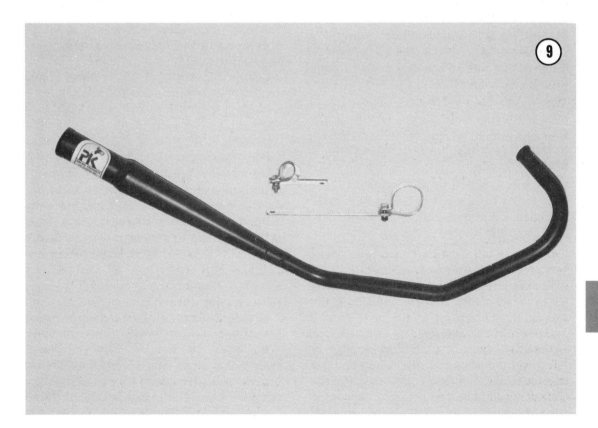

9

XR, the up-style, the down-style, and the HP pipe, which is a down-style exhaust. This last pipe should be used for competition only, since its noise level is higher than either of the other two. For late model XR's, either an up- or down-style pipe is available.

Regardless of which pipe is chosen, it will be necessary to rejet the carburetor before any actual performance gains are realized.

Normally, when a more efficient exhaust system has been installed, the engine will run slightly leaner. However, the XR75 is frequently sold with the carburetor jetted somewhat richer than it should be. While this means that the bike isn't developing full power, this is probably done to prevent the owner/rider from frying his engine — slightly rich engines will run somewhat cooler than correctly jetted or lean ones. But the performance builder wants the maximum available power, so an incorrectly adjusted carburetor is one of the most important areas of concern.

Begin by taking a high speed plug reading. Run the bike in either second or third gear, in the upper portion of the power band, for 2-300 meters. This means that the mixture going to the engine will be almost totally controlled by the main jet. After 200 meters or so, pull the clutch in and, without allowing the rpm to drop off, turn the ignition off.

Drift the bike to a halt and remove the plug. Normally, after the installation of a performance exhaust system, the electrode should be white-gray, indicating a lean condition. However, remembering that the XR may have been preset to run a little fat, you may get a correct reading (light gray) or even a rich (black) condition, even after the installation of your performance exhaust.

Once the plug reading has been made, correction of the main jet size may be done.

Midrange response on the Keihin is controlled by the jet needle, needle jet, and air jet portion of the carburetion circuitry. It must be evaluated, in the absence of a dyno, by feel. Generally, if the engine blubbers through the midrange, the jet needle clip should be raised one notch, to slightly lean the mixture. Poor acceleration will indicate a rich condition, which may be corrected by lowering the jet needle

clip. This should be the only adjustment necessary to correct the midrange.

Low speed mixture may be slightly rich, which will be indicated by the bike's loading up when the bike is accelerated from an idle. Adjustment of the pilot airscrew may correct this problem. However, if this condition is still indicated, it may be necessary to install a smaller-sized pilot jet.

It must be emphasized that carburetor jetting, particularly if the bike will be raced, is not a one-time affair. It will be necessary, for example, to rejet if the bike is ridden at an altitude higher than that at which the initial jetting was made. Also, whenever any performance improvement is made, or any change to the engine whatsoever, the jetting must be corrected to match the engine's new requirements.

A wise competition rider will learn the art of jetting, and keep, in his toolbox, an assortment of jets and the specialized tools used by professional mechanics to change carb jets quickly and precisely.

Camshaft

Once a pipe has been installed on the XR, the stock camshaft should be changed for a higher-performance part.

Cams exist in a wide variety of configurations, from several different manufacturers.

Most of them are hardwelds — stock cams whose profiles have been built up with welding compound, and then a new profile ground on the built-up lobes — but one, from Yoshimura R&D, is made from blank OEM Honda billets.

Basically, the earlier/later a camshaft opens/closes the valves and the greater the amount of valve lift, the more radical a shaft it may be considered, and the greater the benefits which will be gained at high rpm. With a severely radical shaft, however, an unacceptable amount of power may be lost at lower rpm for the rider who wants low end power.

If the engine is being built for racing-only purposes, and will be ridden by an experienced rider, using the optimum high performance shaft makes sense. But if, on the other hand, the bike will still be used for casual sport purposes, a milder shaft might be a better choice. For example, the Yoshimura R&D cam, with inlet opening/closing at 13/40 degrees, and exhaust opening/closing at 40/13 degrees and a valve lift of 0.274 intake, 0.250 exhaust, would be better suited for general purpose riding than the flat-out racing PK Racing cam (**Figure 10**). The PK shaft opens/closes the intake at 26/51 degrees, the exhaust at 54/28 degrees, with a valve lift of 0.277 inches.

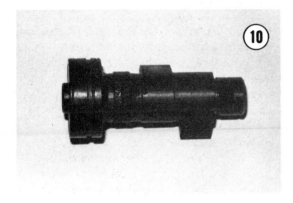

It is easier, at this point, to simply install a bare camshaft, even though full benefits of the cam will not be realized until heavy-duty valve springs are installed. However, stock springs may be used until the head is pulled as part of the later big bore kit installation.

When installing a camshaft, the cam manufacturer's specifications should *always* be followed exactly, even when they depart from stock assembly instructions. Various backyard "experts" will also have the hot word on how to install a cam differently from the manner specified. They should be ignored, since power loss or engine damage is more likely to occur than performance improvements.

If possible, camshaft/springs/big bore kit should all be purchased from the same manufacturer. A manufacturer will generally ensure that this big bore pistons can be installed on an engine with his camshaft without any modification to the piston valve pockets being required. If various components are used, it will be necessary to carefully check piston/valve clearance before the bike is started.

Also, dealing in components from one given manufacturer makes any possible problems fairly easy to deal with. If major problems occur, one maker may be contacted for advice. However, if a cam from maker A is used with valve springs from maker B above a big bore kit from maker C, you can expect little help in the event of trouble — everyone will blame your problems on the other manufacturer.

Moderate benefits will be noticeable with a camshaft installed after carburetor rejetting is accomplished. Full benefits won't be realized until several other modifications to the head are performed at a later stage in engine building.

Carburetion

A high-performance camshaft will, of course, improve the flow and amount of air/fuel mixture entering the engine. So now, the stock carburetor, even though you've rejetted it as best you can, will still be inadequate to the engine's needs.

The stock 20mm Keihin should be removed and replaced with a complete 24mm venturi Keihin carburetor (**Figure 11**) and manifold (**Figure 12**) kit from PK Racing. This will be

9

provided prejetted for your engine, just slightly richer than it should be. Installation of a one-size smaller main jet will generally be the only modification necessary, although the previously outlined plug reading procedure should be made before any changes occur. When the kit is ordered, any changes which have been made to the stock engine (pipe, cam, etc.), plus the altitude the bike will be ridden at, should be specified.

The kit is a bolt-on installation, requiring only a few minutes to put it on the engine. The 24mm carburetor uses the stock throttle linkage.

With a 4mm larger carburetor venturi and inlet passage, a greater amount of fuel/air mixture will be entering the engine, and power will be noticeably increased, particularly when the carburetor change has been accompanied by a high-performance camshaft installation.

A formerly-available modification to the 24mm carburetor was to grind away the cast protrusions in the bellmouth, removal of the choke assembly, and epoxying up of the

passages and mounting holes. Formerly available from PK Racing, this change further improved the flow amount and rate. However, since the work required highly skilled machining, and it was a competition-only modification, when demand for racing parts for the XR75 dropped off PK Racing discontinued the service. It may still be possible to have the work done by an experienced motorcycle dirt performance shop, however.

The restrictive stock air cleaner assembly should be removed and replaced with a K&N or Uni filter (**Figure 13**) which clamps directly to the carburetor's bellmouth. While a filter located out in the open (like the K&N or Uni elements) will require cleaning and servicing more frequently than the stock system, air flow will be significantly bettered.

Big Bore Kits

No single horsepower increase will be as immediately noticeable as increasing the engine's displacement. This will give improvements throughout the engine's powerband, without

either changing the reliability or the maintenance ease of the engine.

The easiest and least expensive of the two ways of upping displacement on the XR75 involves installing a big bore kit. Various kits exist for the machine. Before choosing one, it is advisable to consider the potential uses of the bike. If it will be raced, the limitations of the most popular class in the rider's area must be taken into account. For example, a frequent limitation on displacement is 83cc's. So, if the bike is planned to run in this class, building a larger engine is pointless.

PK Racing makes big bore kits for the pre-1977 XR's which increase total displacement to 79, 80, 81 and 82.5cc's. These kits **(Figure 14)** consist of a new diecast piston, wrist pin, rings, clips and , when needed, a larger head gasket.

Installation consists of removing the head and cylinder, following stock disassembly instructions. The cylinder liner is bored to the instruction-specified new dimension by any competent motorcycle machine shop. The piston is then installed on the connecting rod and the engine reassembled.

Kits are available for the late-model XR75's which give an increased displacement of 79, 79.5, 80 and 81cc's. Disassembly/modification/reassembly procedures are the same as for the earlier models.

With these kits installed, compression is increased to 11.5:1, so care must be taken to run only the finest premium gas in the engine.

A second manufacturer of big bore kits is Yoshimura R&D. They offer two kits for the early model XR75 which increase the displacement to either 80 or 81cc's. The kit requires the same work as the PK Racing kit, and compression is increased to around 10.5:1.

For the late model XR's, Yoshimura offers a slipper piston kit, which will up displacement to 83cc's. A "slipper" piston has certain lower portions cut away, to reduce friction and weight. This 50.5mm diameter piston uses two pistons only. Consequently, there will be greater blow-by into the combustion chamber. This piston kit is intended for racing use *only*.

For those who want a still larger displacement, a PK Racing 98cc big bore kit **(Figure 15)** may be installed. This kit requires complete disassembly of the engine. The stock cylinder liner is punched out and the cylinder itself bored. A larger liner is then installed. The cases themselves must have the spigot bore diameter

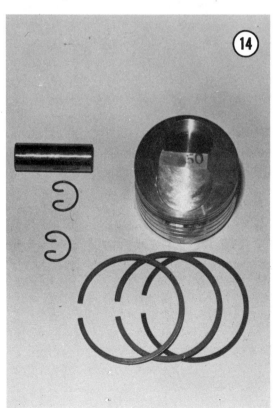

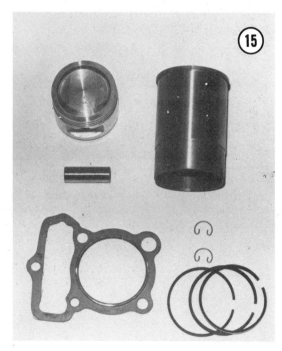

increased to allow for the oversize liner. Once modification is complete, reassembly is to standard instructions.

While the engine is disassembled, the heavy-duty valve springs specified by the camshaft manufacturer should be installed. With the PK Racing cam, their own springs should be used (**Figure 16**). With Yoshimura or other camshaft manufacturers, generally heavy-duty S&W valve springs are recommended. Under no circumstances should these valve springs be shimmed to any degree more than that specified (if at all) by the manufacturer.

With the increased displacement and compression, engine heat will also increase. Heat is the enemy of engine life, so it is highly recommended that a PK Racing oil cooler (**Figure 17**) be installed on any big bore XR75. On the super-large 98cc engine, or on the later-staged stroker engine, the cooler is an absolute necessity. In addition to decreasing oil temperature by 20-30 degrees, use of an oil cooler also increases oil capacity by about one pint.

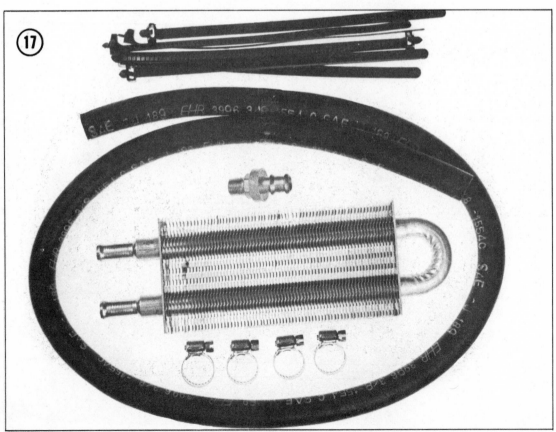

Lightened Crank

With a larger bore and increased power, the next stage is to install a lightened crankshaft (**Figure 18**). The stock crankshaft is disassembled, the weight of the throws cut down, and the assembly put back together. It's available on an exchange basis from PK Racing. Not only will this reduce strain on the lower end bearings, but the engine will rev more rapidly and to a higher rpm than previously allowable.

Ignition

An XR75 engine, modified as already outlined, now can rev much higher than stock. However, as the rpm's increase, the stock ignition system, never more than adequate under normal usage, will now be a drawback. Points bounce will occur at peak rpm, causing irregular firing and loss of needed power.

The solution is to remove the ignition system and replace it with a Motoplat CDI ignition (**Figure 19**).

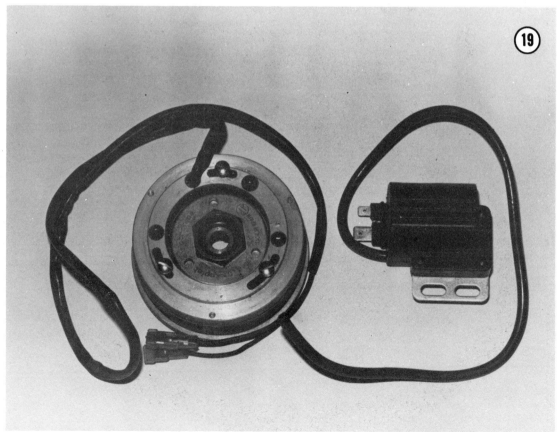

9

This is not an add-on system — the stock alternator, regualator, points assembly, and coil come off and are completely discarded.

The Motoplat CDI is a bolt-on, in place of the stock alternator assembly. Firing is now regulated by magnetic pulse between two non-touching contacts. Not only is spark output almost trebled with the Motoplat, but the system may be set correctly once and thereafter forgotten, since there is no appreciable wear on any of the components. Since this is an expensive system, it is recommended for installation only on competition machines.

Cam Tower/Camshaft

Once again, as the engine's capability to produce power at higher and higher rpm's, stock parts, and now performance parts, prove inadequate.

The stock camshaft bearing tower and camshaft should be removed at this point, and replaced with a PK Racing needle bearing cam tower and camshaft (**Figure 20**). The camshaft has the same profile as the standard PK shaft, but its base is cut to fit into the needle bearing tower.

Not only will the engine be capable of greater rpm, but one mechanical problem characteristic of the XR75 will be prevented from occuring — when, at sustained racing rpm, oil pressure is lost, the oil layer between the cam and the stock carrier is not maintained. With lubrication lost, the cam seizes in the carrier. At the very least, the camshaft is ruined and major engine damage will probably result.

While this modification will produce slight benefits with the engine modified as already outlined, with the next benefit, it becomes a necessity.

The only drawback to the needle bearing tower, of course, is that the owner is thereafter restricted to using the PK Racing camshaft — if that is a drawback.

Stroker Crankshaft

One of the most satisfactory ways to improve performance is to increase displacement by enlarging the engine's stroke.

Stroking, rather than boring an engine, will give a more responsive engine, one which runs harder and which develops far more torque at lower rpm. Its sole drawback is that it is

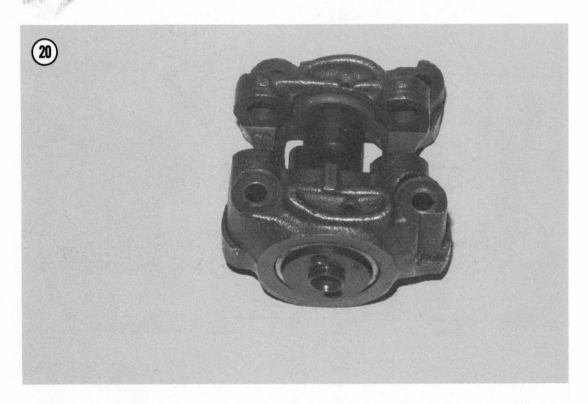

significantly more expensive than installing a big bore kit.

The PK Racing stroker crankshaft (**Figure 21**) will up the engine's stroke from 41.4 centimeters to 46.1 centimeters. The kit consists of a repinned crankshaft (your stock crank must be provided on an exchange basis), a polished connecting rod, a new, shorter stroker piston and piston hardware.

Using the smallest diameter stroker piston, engine displacement with the stroker crank installed will be 81cc's. Varying size pistons are available, giving displacements of 82, 83, 84, 85 and 93cc's. The cylinder liner must, of course, be rebored to accomodate these larger-than-stock pistons.

Installation of the crank, once the engine has been disassembled and the cylinder bored, is extremely simple. No modification to the cases is required. The stock lower end is more than strong enough to accept the high performance assembly, and the reliability of the engine is not affected.

Headwork

Even with a superior cam, exhaust system, carburetor, and air filtration system, optimum performance of the head will not be gained until it has been ported.

In theory, head porting is extremely simple, involving only slow and careful recontouring of the intake and exhaust ports to provide better mixture flow. However, an inexperienced performance builder who roots around with a Dremel tool is probably going to decrease available performance and possibly ruin the head completely.

Since some improvements may be made on two-stroke engine ports by amateurs, frequently the owner of an XR75 will see his friends working on their two-strokes and assume that he can do likewise. Four-stroke engine porting is far more exact and complex than on the simpler two-strokes, and should not be attempted by anyone other than an experienced porting service, such as PK Racing.

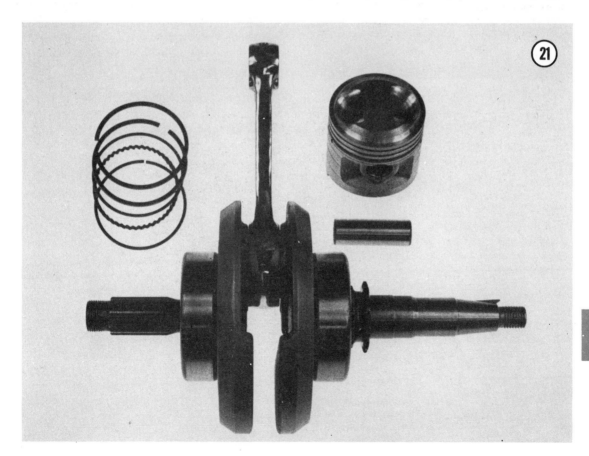

Their standard porting job (**Figure 22**) not only involves increasing the inlet ports to match the 24mm manifold used with the larger Keihin carburetor, enlarging the exhaust port to mate with the exhaust pipe, but a careful removal of the valve guide and supportive casting in the inlet passage (**Figure 23**). In addition, gentle reshaping of the passageways is done.

For riders who need a porting job done for specific competition purposes, PK also provides custom porting work.

After porting, a careful valve job is done before the head is returned. PK Racing uses stock valves and guides, feeling that they are more than strong enough for even severe competition.

For those who want the ultimate, however, Yoshimura R&D offers a set of lightened and polished valves for the XR, in standard dimensions. Installation of oversize valves is not necessary for even racing purposes.

One area on the XR which the owner/racer should be aware of is the intake valve seats. These are very soft and, particularly under the high rpm hammering of competition, will quickly soften and widen out. This widening will produce a significant loss of power — the bike will run as if the front brake is perpetually on.

The owner should become used to removing his XR's head every few races to examine the valve seats. If bad, they should be reground, using the specified stock angles, but as narrow as possible.

Five-Speed Gearbox

Early, four-speed XR75's may have their gearboxes updated to match the newer models with the addition of a five-speed gear cluster (**Figure 24**). This assembly, which replaces the stock transmission assembly (shafts, gears, shifter forks, etc.) and will give a higher first gear for faster starts and a slightly lower top gear for better top speed.

Two manufacturers offer close ratio clusters — Yoshimura R&D and PK Racing. Both gear sets are high quality and manufactured in Japan.

Some riders have considered buying the late-model OEM XR75 five-speed cluster and in-

stalling it in their early model machines. However, the later parts assembly cannot be made to fit in the early transmission cavity.

Clutch

For normal riding purposes the stock Honda XR75 clutch and springs are more than strong enough. However, for competition purposes or when the stock components are worn out, they should be replaced with a Barnett Tool & Engineering heavy duty clutch pack (**Figure 25**). This set of plates is installed to stock specifications. The only problem which might be encountered is that the initial clutch adjustment must be made carefully, to prevent the plates from dragging slightly when cold.

For more positive hookups, PK Racing clutch springs should replace the stock springs. A backyard improvement for stock springs involves shimming them slightly with small washers. However, this increases the probability of coilbind and insufficient disengagement, causing increased clutch plate wear.

Gearing

Gearing must be adjusted to individual riding conditions and to the track. A serious competitor would be advised to experiment with various-sized rear sprockets, which are available with from 42-50 teeth from either PK Racing or Circle Industries. Even after a rider's personal preference has been found, it is advisable to keep one or two variations on hand in your toolbox in order to perform on the spot gearing changes at any given track.

The stock 14-tooth countershaft sprocket may be changed for a replacement sprocket, geared anywhere from 12-15 teeth, from PK Racing.

Most riders find that, with the increased rpm and therefore top end of a performance engine, a 12 or 13 tooth countershaft sprocket may be used for improved low end power.

Under the stress of racing the rear drive chain will be stressed far more severely than normal. Chain wear will be reduced by installing a spring-loaded PK Racing chain tensioner, which is installed on the swing arm and runs on the lower chain row between the countershaft and rear sprockets.

Engine Break In and Gasoline

As each performance improvement is made and the bike reassembled, the engine should be

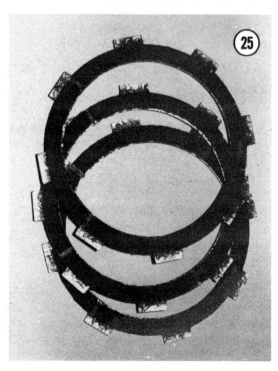

9

broken in carefully. A high-quality 20-50 weight oil, such as that available from Castrol, Kendall, or Valvoline, should be used in place of the stock specified oil.

The bike should be ridden rather moderately for the first two or three hours, rather than wide open. The old myth that a bike should be broken in as it is ridden is wrong — break a bike in hard and it is almost certainly going to break period, or at least be seriously worn with very few miles on it.

It is not a bad idea, after adding internal engine improvements, to start the bike, warm it up and then shut it down without riding the machine. Change the oil immediately to ensure that no filings or other contaminants which may have fallen in the lower end will circulate in the engine.

With a high-compression, high-performance engine, care should be taken, as mentioned previously, to use only the best high-quality premium gas.

It is advisable to buy gas for the XR75 at a busy, top-quality gas station in a metropolitan area. Frequently, riders buy gas at the last station before the boondocks. These small gas stations may have contaminated or otherwise bad gasoline. Where the stock XR75 will run any kind of gas with no problem more annoying than a loss of power, a high-compression, high performance engine is liable to blow running on bad gas.

Care should also be taken that the gas is put in a clean container. Gas should not be stored for any length of time, both because of deterioration and for safety reasons. For the same reason, if the bike has been allowed to sit for a period of time, the gas in the tank should be dumped and a fresh supply used.

OVERALL

Once built to the desired point, the now high-performanced XR75 provides not only a surprisingly quick and fun machine to ride, but a good training mount for a race-ready-except-for-size rider. Performing your own modifications whenever possible and practical, plus maintaining and rebuilding the machine, gives added knowledge and confidence to the owner/rider. Even though the XR75 may no longer be king of the race circuit, it still remains an exceptionally quick and reliable machine — in some ways, still the best of the mini-motorcycles.

Table 1   SOURCES

Manufacturer	Services
Barnett Tool & Engineering 4915 Pacific Blvd. Vernon, Calif. 90058	Heavy duty clutch kits
Bassani Manufacturing 3726 E. Miraloma Anaheim, Calif. 92806	Exhaust pipes, spark arrester
Circle Industries 17901 Arenth Ave. Industry, Calif. 91748	Sprockets
Number One Products 4931 N. Encinita Ave. Temple City, Calif. 91780	Shocks, fork springs, damper kits
PK Racing Products 507 N. Azusa Ave. La Puente, Calif. 91744	High performance engine components, porting, custom engine building, tires, shocks
Pro Fab 3185 Airway Ave. No. C Costa Mesa, Calif. 92626	Custom frames, swing arms
S&W Engineered Products 2616 W. Woodland Dr. Anaheim, Calif. 92801	Shocks, fork springs
Yoshimura R&D 5517 Cleon Ave. North Hollywood, Calif. 91601	Engine components

9

INDEX

A

Air filter 27

B

Backfiring 9
Big bore kits 134-136
Brake cams 31
Brakes
  Cable 99-100
  Description 99
  Drum 101-102
  Lining 100-101
  Troubleshooting 9
Breaker points 25-26

C

Cables 31
Camshaft 49-51, 132-133, 138
Camshaft chain 35
Carburetor
  Adjustments 89-90
  Basic principles 88-89
  Cleaning and inspection 92-93
  Disassembly/assembly 91-92
  Performance improvement 133-134
  Removal and installation 90-91
  Tune-up adjustment 27-28
Clutch
  Adjustment 33-35
  Disassembly, inspection, and installation 60-62
  Performance improvement 141
  Troubleshooting 9
Compression test 22
Connecting rods 52-56
Crankcase disassembly/assembly 68-78
Crankshaft 137, 138-139
Cylinder 51-52
Cylinder head .40-47
Cylinder head nuts 20-21

D

Drive chain 31, 35-36, 102-103

E

Engine
  Break-in 86
  Camshaft and rocker assemblies 49-51
  Cooling 38
  Crankcase 68-78
  Cylinder 51-52
  Cylinder head .40-47
  Oil pump 62-63
  Performance improvement 130-142
  Piston and connecting rods 52-56
  Piston rings 56-57
  Principles of operation 38, 39
  Removal and installation 40
  Service in frame 38-40
  Specifications 87
  Troubleshooting 9
  Valves and valve seats 47-49
Engine number 5
Exhaust system 95, 130-132

F

Footpegs 119
Forks, front 31-32, 112-116, 126-127
Frame .119-121, 128
Frame serial number 5
Fuel system
  Carburetor 88-93
  Fuel shutoff valve 93
  Lines 36

G

Gasoline 141-142
Gearbox, 5-speed 140-141
Gearing 141
Gearshift drum and forks 85-86
General information 1-5

H

Handlebars 108
Headwork 139-140

I

Idle, rough 8
Ignition system
  Checks and adjustments 93-94
  Performance improvement 137-138
  Timing 25

K

Kickstand 118-119

L

Lubricants and fuel 28, 141-142
Lubrication (see Maintenance)

M

Magneto 24-25, 65-68
Maintenance (also see Tune-up)
  Brake cams 31
  Cables 31
  Camshaft chain 35
  Cleaning solvents 28
  Clutch adjustment 33-35
  Drive chain .31, 35-36
  Engine oil change 28, 30-31
  Fasteners 37

10

Forks, front 31-32
Fuel lines 36
General inspection 28
Lubricants 28
Routine checks 28-30
Service intervals 33
Spokes 37
Steering head bearings 31
Storage 37
Throttle operation 32
Tire inspection 30
Tire pressure 28
Wheel bearings 31
Wheels and tires 36-37
Misfiring   8

O

Oil, engine 28-30
Oil pump 62-63
Overheating   8

P

Parts replacement   4
Performance improvement
Engine 130-142
General information 122-124
Overall 142
Sources 142
Suspension .124-130
Piston 52-56
Piston rings 56-57
Piston seizure 8-9
Power loss   8
Primary drive 57-60

R

Rocker assemblies 49-51

S

Safety procedures   4
Serial numbers   5
Service procedures 2-4
Shifter mechanism 63-65
Shocks, performance improvement 124-126
Shocks, rear 116-118
Solvents, cleaning 28
Spark plug 22-23
Specifications, engine 87
Specifications and dimensions, general 2, 3
Spokes 37
Starting problems   8
Steering head 108-112
Steering head bearings 31
Storage 37
Suspension
Forks, front 112-116
Performance improvement 124-130

Shocks, rear .116-118
Swing arm 118
Troubleshooting 10
Swing arm 118, 128

T

Throttle operation 32
Timing 25
Tires 28-30, 103-107, 128-130
Tools
Broken screws or bolts 19
Fasteners 11-13
Frozen nuts and screws, removing 18-19
Ignition gauge 16
Impact driver 16
Pliers 14-15
Screwdrivers .13-14
Spoke wrench 17
Stripped threads 19
Tire lever 16
Tune-up and troubleshooting tools 17-18
Wrenches 15-16
Transmission
Disassembly/assembly (1975-1976) 82-84
Disassembly/assembly (1977 and later) 84-85
Gearshift drum and forks 85-86
General information 78-81
Troubleshooting 10
Troubleshooting
Brakes   9
Clutch   9
Emergency troubleshooting   7
Operating problems 8-9
Operating requirements 6-7
Starting problems   8
Suspension 10
Transmission 10
Tune-up
Air filter 27
Breaker point adjustment and magneto
timing 25-26
Breaker point replacement 26
Breaker point inspection and cleaning 26
Carburetor adjustment 27-28
Compression test 22
Cylinder head nuts 20-21
Magneto 24
Spark plug 22-23
Valve clearance adjustment 21-22

V

Valve clearance adjustment 21-22
Valves and valve seats 47-49

W

Wheel, front 96-97, 128
Wheel, rear 97-98
Wheel bearings 31

NOTES

MAINTENANCE LOG

DATE	TYPE OF SERVICE	COST	REMARKS
6-28-80	oil change		

Owner-Service...
for U.S. Cars and Trucks

Clymer's professionally-written car manuals are a must for every do-it-yourself car owner. Expert text by top technical writers is illustrated by hundreds of photos, drawings, and diagrams. The use of special tools and test equipment is avoided wherever possible. When necessary, these items are illustrated in actual use or alone. Jobs that are not within the ability of the owner/ mechanic are pointed out and service referred to a dealer or repair shop.

†Manuals preceded by a dagger (†) cover lubrication, tune-up, and troubleshooting exclusively. All other manuals offer complete maintenance, troubleshooting, tune-up, and overhaul information for hundreds of different models. All titles are available through local bookstores, automotive accessories outlets, or postpaid directly from Clymer Publications.

• *NEW COLOR-IDENTIFIED QUICK REFERENCE PAGES* will be included in most new and updated books. The most frequently used specs will be found all together at the front of the book for ready reference — including tune-up specs, fluid capacities, torque settings, light bulb types, tire pressures, adjustments, and more.

• *NEW TAB IDENTIFIERS* will be included in all new and updated books to help readers locate chapters and sections easily.

AMC PACER, HORNET, AND GREMLIN,
1971-1977 .... (A129) $9.00

CAMARO, 1967-1978 .... (A136) $9.00

CHEVETTE, 1976-1978 .... (A134) $9.00

†CHEVROLET CAR MAINTENANCE, 1966-1977 (A137) $7.00

†CHEVROLET & GMC FWD MAINT., 1967-1977 (A230) $7.00

†CHEVROLET & GMC VAN AND PICKUP
MAINTENANCE, 1967-1977 .... (A240) $7.00

CORVETTE, 1963-1976 .... (A146) $10.00

DODGE CAR MAINTENANCE, 1968-1976 ...... (A153) $7.00

†DODGE & PLYMOUTH FWD MAINTENANCE,
1965-1975 .... (A231) $7.00

†DODGE & PLYMOUTH VAN AND PICKUP
MAINTENANCE, 1965-1975 .... (A241) $7.00

†FORD CAR MAINTENANCE, 1969-1976 .... (A170) $7.00

†FORD FWD MAINTENANCE, 1969-1975 .... (A232) $7.00

†FORD VAN AND PICKUP MAINT., 1969-1977 (A242) $7.00

†INTERNATIONAL (IHC) FWD & PICKUP
MAINTENANCE, 1962-1975 .... (A233) $7.00

†JEEP FWD MAINTENANCE, 1969-1975 .... (A234) $7.00

MUSTANG, 1964-1973 .... (A167) $9.00

MUSTANG II, 1974-1976 .... (A169) $9.00

PINTO, 1971-1976 .... (A171) $9.00

†PLYMOUTH CAR MAINTENANCE, 1967-1976 (A179) $7.00

VEGA, 1971-1976 .... (A135) $9.00

CLYMER PUBLICATIONS

12860 Muscatine Street
P.O. Box 20
Arleta, California 91331